Speaking the Truth in Love

A True Account of Events
and Concerns Related to The
Local Churches 1987-1989

John Ingalls

Stephen Isitt

ARPress
45 Dan Road Suite 5
Canton MA 02021
Hotline: 1(888) 821-0229
Fax: 1(508) 545-7580

Ordering Information:
Quantity sales. Special discounts are available on quantity purchases by corporations, associations, and others. For details, contact the publisher at the address above.

Printed in the United States of America.

ISBN-13:	Softcover	979-8-89676-279-9
	eBook	979-8-89676-280-5
	Hardback	979-8-89676-281-2

Library of Congress Control Number: 2025907043

Table of Contents

CONCLUSION 133

OUR WAY FOR THE FUTURE 136

APPENDIX

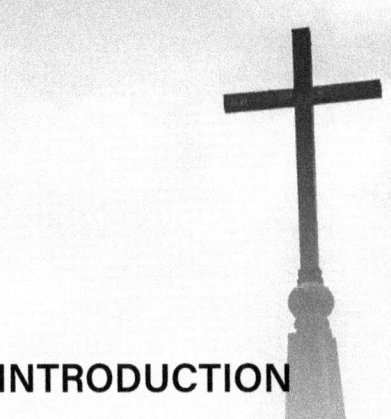

INTRODUCTION

Having been a close observer of the tumultuous events that have transpired and the change of course that has taken place during the past few years in the local churches under the leadership of Witness Lee, and having been myself an intimate co-worker of Witness Lee's and an elder in the local churches for more than twenty-five years, I feel it is appropriate and indeed obligatory for me to relate an account of my own observations, inward exercises, and responses. I do this for the sake of a historical record and for the benefit of any who may be profited thereby. My burden is not to write exhaustively, for that would be too tedious for the reader, but to give an objective and as accurate an account as possible of the main concerns and burdens that have brought me to my present position and of the related events that have transpired over the past few years.

Moreover, many things have been spoken in recent elders' meetings by Brother Witness Lee and his co-workers that totally misrepresent the facts and contain many untruths. Motives and intentions are imputed to us that we never imagined, not to say practiced. We are being called despicable names and are being displayed in the worst light. But we do not desire to stoop to the level of name calling, pejorative epithets, or blatant vindication. We would like to speak the facts sincerely before God in Christ. May the Lord judge us in every attitude and action, as indeed He has continually been doing with all of us. We commit ourselves to Him. We desire to give a true account of the facts and our intentions and let the readers judge.

We certainly never imagined that we would pass through the experiences and conflict that we have in recent years. We loved the Lord's recovery and gave everything for it for over a quarter of a century. It was this love and investment of our lives that compelled us to respond and speak out. We had seen something that was exceedingly precious, and it was in jeopardy. Moreover, we were concerned that the Lord's testimony would be brought into shame and disgrace and suffer great damage. Sadly, our fears have eventualized. But we believe the Lord will still go on to recover and rebuild. I will now proceed with the account and my testimony.

PART ONE

EARLY STAGES

August – September 1987

In the summer of 1987, I began to be concerned for the first time about some of the things taking place under the direction of the Living Stream Ministry Office. The things that were done and promoted in the high school training in Irving, Texas, in August 1987 greatly disturbed me, especially knowing that Philip Lee, the manager of the LSM office, was giving direct instructions and "fellowship" for the training's execution. The despising attitude that was instilled in the young people towards the elders of their churches was appalling. This was manifested in the arrogance and rudeness with which they addressed a good number of elders who were present, exhorting them to be baptized again. I was there and saw it. But then, learning afterwards there was some amount of repentance for this accompanied with an apology to the elders, I was somewhat comforted. However, many young people who attended were afterward very disappointed and discouraged in their Christian life, and some were seriously damaged in their attitude toward the Lord and the church as a result of that training, some of them it seems irreparably. The young people in Anaheim suffered a severe blow.

In the following month, September 1987, due to my health, and also due to a burden to fellowship with Bill Mallon, a co-worker with whom I had an intimate relationship for twenty-four years, I decided to go to Atlanta, Georgia, for a two-week period of rest and fellowship. Bill had recently passed through sore trials and sufferings, and I hoped that our fellowship could render comfort and encouragement to him. We drove up to the nearby mountains and had a number of days opening to one another.

At that time, I was entirely supportive to Brother Witness Lee and his ministry and work related to the "new way" that was being promoted. I therefore did my utmost to persuade Bill to visit Taiwan and participate in the full-time training. I felt that this might be the answer to his need. On four separate occasions during those days, I attempted to convince Bill to take this step, but he steadfastly refused, affirming that he was not free or clear to do that.

During that time Bill explained to me how he had suffered in various ways by events that had transpired in recent months in the churches and in the work in the Southeast. I came away from our talks with one deep impression: Philip Lee was becoming increasingly involved in spiritual things concerning the Lord's work, the churches, the elders, and the co-workers. I had already noticed this in Irving, Texas the preceding month. This, I felt, was completely untenable, incompatible with his position and person, and intolerable. Philip Lee was employed by his father, Witness Lee, to be the business manager of his office and was reportedly instructed to deal only with business affairs. He was totally unqualified both in position and character to touch spiritual matters related to the work of the Lord and the churches. I became alarmed and began to fear for the Lord's testimony. With this burden I determined upon my return to Anaheim to fellowship with Godfrey Otuteye, who then was involved in coordinating with Philip Lee in the Living Stream Office. I wanted to frankly ask him about Philip's role, expressing my alarm and concern.

Godfred had been an elder in the church in Irvine, California, for close to ten years, and had recently been appointed as an elder in Anaheim by Brother Witness Lee. Thus, we had been put into a position of more intimate fellowship and coordination. I had known Godfred since 1972 and over the years had numerous occasions of fellowship with him. I respected him for his genuineness, wisdom, and devotion to the Lord. Hence, upon returning from Atlanta on Sept. 22, 1987,

I made an appointment for dinner with Godfred on September 25, Friday evening.

We sat together in the restaurant, and after some general conversation, I said to him in a serious tone, "Godfred, I would like to ask you a question. Would you please tell me who Philip Lee is? It seems that he is being promoted and is going altogether too far in his involvement in the spiritual side of the work, greatly overstepping his position as a business manager. Have you noticed this? I myself could never agree with this."

It seemed that my question took him by surprise. We had never discussed these matters before. He hesitated a few moments. Then, in a very grave tone, he replied, "John, the situation is very serious." If he was surprised by my question, I was somewhat taken aback by his answer. Godfred continued, "I have seen and heard many things in the Living Stream Office in recent months. I cannot go into detail, but I can tell you there is much that is very serious and very wrong." Then I began to be more alarmed and concerned. Godfred fully agreed that Philip Lee's involvement in the work was way out of line, but he indicated that there were more serious things than that.

Two days later, on Sept. 27, the Lord's Day, as we met in the Elders' Room before the morning meeting on Ball Road, Godfred had a few moments alone with me, and he said, "John, it is very timely that you opened up to me the other night. Let me tell you that the whole situation is sick and corrupt. I have seen and heard too much." Then I knew that we were really in trouble, though he did not mention any details or any names.

A SHOCKING DEVELOPMENT

September 1987

On the following Tuesday, Sept. 29th, Godfred left for a business trip to Europe. On the next day, Wednesday, Sept. 30th, I received a telephone call from a sister who had a prominent position in the Living Stream Ministry Office, asking if she could see me that night. I consented. That evening she sat in my living room and with tears opened her heart to me. She had served sacrificially and faithfully for many years in the LSM office, and now she said she could not tolerate anymore the gross misconduct that was being perpetrated upon some and especially upon her. I had been acquainted with this sister for many years and knew her to be faithful, upright, and trustworthy; therefore, I took her word very seriously. I was amazed that she could put up with such conduct for so long. She stated that she tolerated it only for the sake of Brother Lee and his ministry. She said that she had no other recourse but to resign. I confirmed her intention.

That conversation utterly shocked me. I deeply felt that something must be done to acquaint Brother Lee with the situation and to let him know that we would not tolerate it. I obtained Godfred's telephone number in Europe and called him as soon as the difference in time zones permitted, telling him the things that had come to my ears. Godfred listened and said that he already knew it. I was amazed. That night I considered what could be done. That we had to go to Brother Lee I was certain.

CONSIDERING HOW TO BRING THE PROBLEMS BEFORE BROTHER LEE

October – November 1987

The grievous conduct reported by the sister from the LSM office had a precedent that we were well aware of. Ten years previously there had been reports of similar incidents in the LSM office confirmed by several eyewitnesses. This compounded the serious nature of the case. I felt that it was more than a local matter, since the LSM was part of the work of Brother Lee, and the ministry of the office affected churches everywhere. Therefore, I believed it to be reasonable and advisable for a few prominent co-workers who were aware of the history of the case and who were respected by Brother Lee to approach him and inform him of the matter. (Actually, the principle of a group of brothers conferring with Brother Lee about a serious problem, a crisis, in the local churches had already been practiced on March 30, 1978, when a group of brothers – four from Texas, one from Los Angeles, and Gene Gruhler and I from Anaheim –went to see him in his home.) The next day I called Godfred again in Europe and presented my thoughts to him. He agreed.

During the next few days I telephoned several brothers, co-workers whom I respected and trusted and with whom I had served for many years. They were aware of the incidents ten years previously. I informed them in a general way of the current situation and proposed to them that we go together to Brother Lee in an effort to impress him with the gravity of the case and to clear it up. It was the first week of October

1987. We felt we should pray more and consider further what to do, since at that time Brother Lee was out of the country, in Taiwan.

One of the brothers I sought to contact and confer with was Ray Graver, an elder in the church in Irving, Texas, and the manager of the LSM branch office there. I called him in Texas and proposed that I come to see him in Irving. It was thought, however, for us to meet in Irving would attract too much attention; so we settled on meeting midway in El Paso, Texas. This decision is being censured now as a plan for a secret meeting, as if that in itself is evil and a conspiracy. But I fail to see anything wrong with this. It was with a pure motive and desire and certainly was not a plot to draw him into a conspiracy to overthrow anyone's ministry. Ray was quite willing to do this until Benson Phillips, another co-worker and elder in Irving, Texas, who was then in Taiwan, advised him against it. Had Benson been in Irving, I would have sought to speak with him also. I enjoyed a very good and close relationship with both Ray and Benson for many years.

In those days I had further fellowship with Godfred and with some of the brothers we had contacted, with whom we had intimate fellowship through the years concerning the Lord's work. We realized that the spiritual condition of the churches. In those days I had further fellowship with Godfred and with some of the brothers we had contacted, with whom we had intimate fellowship through the years concerning the Lord's work. We realized that the spiritual condition of the churches throughout the United States and in other places, generally speaking, was very poor, very low. We searched for the reason. Something was radically wrong. The Lord's blessing was not among us. Life was at a very low ebb. In a number of places there was considerable discord and dissension, and instead of a steady increase in numbers, there was a steady decrease. We began to realize then that there were practices and tendencies among us that we had never considered before. And, we ourselves as well as others were responsible, having participated in these. But we had not seen clearly or realized previously what was being done. Thus, we began to come to some conclusions.

I believe that the first was that the ministry was being given a place above the churches. It was being too highly exalted and emphasized, so that it became imperative for every church now to manifest that they were "for the ministry" and to "serve the ministry". It was no longer, as we were often told, that the ministry was for the churches and that only the churches should be built up; rather the churches now should be for the ministry, and the ministry was being built up. We felt that we should voice such a concern to brother Lee.

About the second week of October, we began to fellowship with Dan Towle, an elder in the church in Fullerton and a trainer from the full-time training in Taipei, who was attempting to give direction and help to the fifty or sixty full-timers who had moved from Taipei to Orange County. To his great frustration, the full-timers were taken over by the LSM office and its management, and were charged to do construction and yard work over an extended period of time to the neglect of their gospel preaching. Dan had also heard some things concerning misconduct and irregularities related to the ministry office that greatly upset him, and he had serious concerns as we did for the Lord's recovery. At one point he told me that he considered to resign from the work and to leave. We confirmed his feeling that the situation was indeed serious.

Godfred, Dan, and I came together a few times, joined also by Ken Unger on a couple of occasions to fellowship about the situation and what should be done. Ken Unger, who was an elder in Huntington Beach, had himself also become very concerned. We conferred about our burden to speak with Brother Lee, mentioning a number of our concerns that involved aberrations of truth and practice. When we touched the matter of the full-time training in Taipei, Dan responded by saying that if you touch the FTTT, you touch Brother Lee himself, and according to his observation of Brother Lee's practice, Brother Lee will consider you if you become in his eyes a problem, and then he will proceed to carry out his burden without you. Godfred confirmed this by saying that he had the same realization, that Brother Lee considers anyone who criticizes him a troublemaker and will consider whether or not that one is expendable. This was indeed a most serious consideration concerning Brother Lee. But we did not care to maintain any position or standing for ourselves. We felt that for the Lord's sake and for the sake of all the brothers and sisters, we must open our hearts to Brother Lee, no matter what it cost us.

As we spoke of our various concerns it was evident that Dan was growing increasingly uneasy. Regarding the FTTT he said, "I was one of the co-conspirators in that." He felt that we were going too far and desired to withdraw from further fellowship. At this point we felt that it would be useful for the brothers we had contacted to come together to fellowship and pray in preparation for going to see Brother Lee, so that we would be clear concerning the issues we would present to him. Moreover, we believed it would be best not to create any stir among the saints or other elders by doing this openly; so we sought some place where we could all meet privately. This was by no means a conspiracy, as we are being charged. At no time did we ever meet with the purpose of plotting to overthrow Brother Lee and his ministry. That is utterly ridiculous. We never had such a thought – the Lord can testify for us. A private meeting or a secret meeting does not constitute a conspiracy. A conspiracy takes form from the content of the meeting. Is it a conspiracy to pray and fellowship together in preparation for visiting Brother Lee and opening our hearts in frank fellowship? Of course not. We were very concerned for the saints and sought for an extended period to cover the grave matters from them lest they be distraught and we suffer worse consequences.

One of the brothers then expressed rather strongly that it would be better for just a few brothers, namely those from Anaheim, to confer with Brother Lee instead of the whole group of five or six. Hence, after further consideration, we dropped the whole thought of all the brothers coming together, and decided that just Godfred, Al Knoch, and myself, elders in Anaheim, would go.

By this time Godfred and I felt that we must acquaint Brother Al Knoch with the facts and our deep concerns. We did so, and amidst many tears and great grief Al, who was already very much aware of some problems in the LSM office and could readily discern other difficulties affecting us in Anaheim, agreed to accompany us to see Brother Lee. The time was early November. Brother Lee was still in Taiwan and was not due to return until December 5th, 1987. We felt that we could not adequately or properly discuss such grave issues with him over the phone, and it was not practical for us to make a trip to Taiwan. Therefore, we determined to wait for his return and seek the earliest possible opportunity to speak with him in his presence.

THE CONDITION OF THE
CHURCH IN ANAHEIM

October – November 1987

During this time, we were concerned for the saints in Anaheim and the condition of the church. We had just concluded the gospel "blitz" in Anaheim during the summer training of 1987, when over 3700 were baptized through knocking on doors. There had been a strong effort to follow up the 800 or more who were baptized in Anaheim (the remainder lived in other cities of Orange County and were being cared for by other churches). There were grand scale preparation and follow-up plans with the activity headed up by two brothers, appointed by the church, who gave themselves to the work. The elders also gave themselves to the labor, though I myself was much restricted by my health. But to our dismay many of those who were baptized had disappeared, many rejected any further visits, and the remaining fruit was sparse. Some discouragement set in.

To compound the problem, a good number of saints had reacted against the practice of door-knocking, not openly or actively, but by simply withdrawing from the church life and the meetings. They felt that if that was the way the church was going to take, it was not for them. And indeed the meetings were filled with door-knocking testimonies, and anyone who desired to speak anything else felt he would be out of the "flow". In this kind of atmosphere the life in the church ebbed even further from the already low state. We felt that the vision of Christ and the church that had so captured us at the beginning, over two decades ago, had grown dim or had vanished altogether. Those who were still with us in the church were either doing their best to carry out the visitation of the new ones with the methodology of the new way, or simply felt left out since they either lacked the heart or could not match the demands. All were desperately lacking the nourishing supply of the living word, of the Spirit, and of life. Therefore, we were burdened to give some messages on the Lord's Day to try to renew the vision and supply life. We spoke a number of times from Colossians and Revelation, emphasizing Christ as the tree of life. At one point one of the brothers who was taking the lead among the young people, Chris Leu, said to me, "John, you are going to be in trouble!" He indicated that Brother Lee and other leading ones would not be happy with me, because I was not speaking the same thing as Brother Lee in Taiwan concerning the new way. I told him I could not help that; I had to discharge my burden to meet the need. If for that reason I would be in trouble, then I must be in trouble. We had to care for the saints in our locality regardless of what was being spoken in Taiwan or done in other places. This experience pointed up a fallacy among us – the prevalent concept that everyone must speak what Brother Lee was speaking and conform universally, regardless of the local need. We were aware of that but could not conscientiously follow.

During the months of October and November 1987 the elders in Anaheim met regularly with the other elders in Orange County. We expressed to them our burden, our burden concerning the low condition of the churches and the need for the revival of our vision and some of the basic things of life. Others shared similar things. The Thanksgiving weekend was coming up, and there was to be a young people's conference in the mountains. This was brought up for fellowship, and the question arose concerning who should go to lead the young people. We learned then that one of the trainers from Taiwan had already been encouraged through those serving in the LSM office to come, and in fact he was preparing to come. Most all of the brothers felt strongly and expressed clearly their disagreement with that arrangement, based upon the damage wrought by the high school training in Irving, Texas, in which this particular trainer had a prominent role. The elders asked two brothers among them to telephone this trainer in Taiwan to inform him of the brothers' feeling that someone else should lead the young people in the coming conference. They did so immediately. It was indeed a shock to the brother in Taiwan. It also was a blow to Philip Lee, who presumed to be directing these affairs.

The elders also agreed that for the rest of the saints it would be profitable to come together on Thanksgiving weekend to share some things concerning Christ, the Spirit, life, and the church. All the elders would share the same burden. A few days before the conference was to start Philip Lee met with the full-timers and told them they had no business attending that conference; they should take care of their new ones. It was clear that Philip was absolutely unhappy with our conference. We felt rather that it was most appropriate for the full-timers to bring their new ones to the conference if they were so led. This is the kind of situation we faced.

A few days after the conference, Benson Phillips came to Anaheim from Taiwan and met with the full-timers. Philip Lee, Dan Towle, and Dan Leslie were also present (the latter two had been attempting with difficulty to lead the full-timers in service). Through Benson's fellowship the leadership of Dan Towle and Dan Leslie with the full-timers was officially terminated, and the full-timers were left under the direction of the LSM office. This was a blow to the two Dan's. The full-timers were left in confusion, and serious questions were raised in some of them.

A few days later Benson desired to meet with some of the elders representing churches in the area. A lunch was arranged in a nearby restaurant to be followed by fellowship. Present at the meeting were Benson, Dan Towle, Dan Leslie, Ken Unger, Ned Nossaman, Dick Taylor, Frank Scavo, Godfred Otuteye, Al Knoch, and John Ingalls. During the fellowship the brothers began to question Benson concerning current events with the full-timers and the Living Stream Office and the prospects for the church's relationship with the full-timers. The involvement of the LSM office and its management was a real concern. Benson found it very difficult to answer the brothers' questions and was alarmed at the attitude of the brothers toward the LSM office. He remarked that the atmosphere in Orange County had changed, and he was bothered. We also were greatly bothered.

RECOVERY VERSION
TRANSLATION DEBACLE

October 1987

Over a period of eleven years, from 1974 to 1984, I had worked together with other brothers on the preparation of the text for the Recovery Version of the New Testament. During the greater part of that time, and up to the completion, my coworkers were Bill Duane and Albert Knoch. We worked by ourselves in direct conjunction with Brother Witness Lee, presenting to him our work on each book. Anything to do with the text, any revisions or alterations, were accomplished in direct consultation with Brother Lee. After that he delivered it to the Living Stream Office for all the processes of printing and publication. Hence, in all this work we had no contact whatever with the office.

After the entire New Testament was completed, we anticipated the time when a thorough revision would be made to strengthen various weaknesses in the translation, and to make it more concordant, accurate, and readable. We were informed, however, that the work of revision would be totally headed up by the Living Stream Ministry Office, that is, by its general manager Philip Lee. From past experience and observation we knew that such a relationship would be fraught with great difficulties, and we were full of apprehension. But we had no choice. A room was prepared in the LSM office for this work, and the date for the commencement of the work was set for October 15th.

Kerry Robichaux, a full-time employee of the LSM office was appointed to work with us as a special consultant. he had an advanced degree in linguistics, specializing in Greek; so he was considered a valuable asset to the work. Moreover, he had assisted Brother Lee along with others on the work of the Chinese Recovery Version in Taipei. A Chinese-speaking brother was also appointed to work with us, checking all our work to see that the English revision conformed to the Chinese Recovery Version, which was to be the universal base of other language versions.

On Thursday, October 15, we sat down together in our new facility for the first time and endeavored to lay some groundwork regarding the principles under which we would operate. It was not long before we clashed with Kerry over the guidelines, but we managed to get through and go on. The second day, October 16th, Kerry mentioned some matters regarding the daily schedule which he had received from Philip Lee, with whom he was in continual contact. There was some difficulty over that due to our prior understanding, and Bill Duane proposed that I should be the one to maintain contact with Philip, and not allow room for confusion by both Kerry and I bringing announcements from the office. Relating to the confusion, Bill added, "We should not give any ground for the devil to come in and frustrate our work." Kerry was not happy with Bill's proposal, but we managed to finish the session and arrange to come back the following week.

To my utter amazement I was informed the following day by Godfred, who received a telephone call from Philip, that our work was being immediately terminated, and the translation would be moved to Texas. Kerry had reported what Bill Duane had said to Philip Lee, and Philip blew up, totally misinterpreting what Bill Duane had said, and calling his father in Taiwan to report the whole affair. He believed that Bill had referred to him, Philip Lee, as the Devil, when he said, "We should not give any ground for the devil to come in." Using a Chinese proverb, he said that if you treat the dog evilly, then in effect you render the same treatment to the dog's master, signifying Brother Lee. If you call the general manager of the LSM the Devil, then you call his boss, Brother Lee the same. By this twist of facts and logic, Philip concluded that we were attacking both him and his father. Godfred was appalled and totally disgusted with Philip Lee's reaction and the way the whole affair was being handled. He was outraged, more so than me, considering that we who had been so closely and deeply involved in the work for years and burdened for its final completion were so abruptly being relieved of our responsibility and replaced. He pointed out to me that this was an example of Phillip's untenable, growing influence over the work and over his father.

Early in the morning on the following day, the Lord's Day, Brother Lee called me from Taiwan, and said that he had learned of the problem. He ordered us to stop the work for a week and not continue for a week to allow time to pray and consider what to do. He asked me to pray too. I told Brother Lee over the phone what actually had happened and that it was not at all as he had heard. In any case, Brother Lee felt that to keep the peace there had better be a change. A few days later he had called again to say that he had made the final decision: the work would be moved to Irving, Texas, just as Godfred had been told by Philip Lee. Kerry and others would work there and send their drafts to me, and I would personally render the final review. I acquiesced to this arrangement. It seemed clear that Bill Duane was being excluded from any part in the work. Brother Lee also advised me to use my time to render more help to the church in Anaheim, a matter for which I told him I was burdened.

Fairly speaking, given the parameters of the work under which we were expected to labor, i.e. the ministry office environment with Philip Lee in charge, it would have definitely been necessary sooner or later to make some rearrangement. There would inevitably be friction and unpleasant eruptions. From the beginning I could foresee nothing else. Therefore, for the work to continue in peace Brother Lee would eventually be forced to take some sort of action. I am thankful that it occurred sooner rather than later. For me the burden of the work under such conditions would have been a great strain on my health, and I was not ready to sacrifice my life in that way. (Some brothers have recently asserted that I should have used the opportunity of Brother Lee's telephone calls from Taiwan to share with him over the phone our deep concerns. This I would never do. Such grave considerations required face to face encounters.)

Bill Duane was utterly revulsed upon learning of Philip Lee's reaction and the way the matter was handled. Under such conditions he was happy to be relieved of any further involvement, but saddened that the translation work came to such a conclusion. I continued in the work on the revision, polishing the drafts from Texas and passing them on to Brother Lee, for over a year. Eventually, toward the end of 1988, I felt I should withdraw, and tendered a letter of resignation to Brother Lee on December 3rd. That brought to a close a major era in my life and work.

FACTORS OF PROBLEM
AND CONCERN

Meanwhile we needed to consider many things, analyzing our history to discover the factors which caused our poor condition. In so doing we arrived at numerous other conclusions that concerned us greatly.

1. An excessive emphasis on numbers

We have already referred to the matter of the work and the ministry being promoted and given a place of undue preeminence and centrality. The "burden of the ministry" was that over the years the rate of increase had been decreasing, and a way must be found to preach the gospel and increase the numbers dramatically. This led to an inordinate emphasis on numbers and increase, with a great stress on budgets, goals plans, methods, and ways, coupled with predictions of millions being baptized over a period of several years and guarantees that if we would follow the prescribed way the numbers in the churches would be multiplied many fold. We listened to many messages and viewed many video tapes from Taiwan to this effect. Most of the churches, including Anaheim, dived into the burden with a very good heart to follow and obey, but the fervor was beginning to diminish and many saints were left languishing.

We fully agreed that the gospel should be preached and that we were short of normal healthy increase and the proper gospel preaching, but what could bring this to pass? What was the remedy? We were not so clear. But we began to be very clear that the diagnosis of our real need and the way that was being prescribed were seriously flawed. This was abundantly confirmed not only by the word of God but by Brother Lee's own ministry on many previous occasions. We have seen through his help a vision of God's economy and recovery, and such an emphasis on numbers, increase, budgets, methods, etc., was at great variance with what we had seen. This was not what we had heard from the beginning. This was not what attracted us to the Lord's recovery and brought us into the church life. Some had come out of Christian groups with this very emphasis, still unsatisfied, hungry, seeking rest and nourishment, oneness and true fellowship.

We analyzed our history in this country and saw that every time numbers and increase were stressed serious problems arose, and eventually there was a loss, not a gain. On January 17, 1983, Brother Lee said in a message to the elders which was later printed (entitled Practical Talks to the Elders), "Let us trace a little of our history. The recovery in the United States began in Los Angeles in 1962. For ten years, from 1962 to 1972, I had very little concern. My only burden was to keep pressing on....Then we became careless, or more accurately, distracted. We were distracted from what the Lord had shown us, and turned our attention to the increase. From 1972 there was a tendency to promote numbers, to be occupied with getting the proper place and the proper people. That opened the door for some things to creep in to damage the Lord's recovery....Then I began to say that we must turn our attention away from the increase and come back to the central lane, the lane of life, the lane of God's focus (emphasis ours)".

It was evident that we were embarked upon the same damaging cycle again. We were deviating from God's focus and God's economy. This was undoubtedly the work of the subtle one. We surely needed to return to the lane of life as Brother Lee had stated. We felt that as those who had served with Brother Lee for many years we should speak honestly and faithfully to him concerning this.

2. The Influence and Control of the LSM Office

Another matter that concerned us greatly was the growing influence and control of the LSM office, i.e. Philip Lee) over churches, elders, co-workers, and the full-time training in Taiwan. We had numerous examples of such an intolerable and unscriptural situation. With my own eyes I saw some leading ones reporting to Philip Lee what they were intending to share with a gathering of Orange County young people and ask if he thought that would be all right. I could hardly believe it. Was this the function of a business manager? When I reported this observation to some brothers who had coordinated with Philip Lee and associated with him, they laughed at me and said that that was very common. They were amused by my being startled by this discovery. Godfred even admitted later that he had done the same thing himself: he had suggested that before someone was chosen to lead a young people's conference it should be checked out with Philip. Godfred fully repented of that. Dan Towle remarked that this was our "lifestyle". How far off we were!

Moreover, elders were encouraged to call Philip Lee regarding conferences and many affairs concerning the work and the churches in their areas, asking his advice and who should come to help them. A few places actually practiced this. There are a number of instances of churches and whole areas being cut off by the management of the LSM office from the supply of literature and tapes due to some alleged offense of the elders, regardless of the suffering imposed upon the saints in those churches. When the elders repented in a manner satisfactory to the office, the ban was lifted. Some adjustments, we understand have been made in the administration of the LSM office, but at that time the situation was bad and worsening. The portent for the future was threatening. This was a genuine concern.

3. Aberrational Speaking and Activity in the FTTT

In addition we began to hear reports, see video tapes, and read printed messages published by the Full-time Training in Taipei of some of the things that were being said and done. Now this really alarmed us. Foremost among these was the fact that Philip Lee was the administrator of the training, supposedly only on the business side, but actually exercising supervision in much more than business affairs. He was in daily fellowship with twenty-four of the trainers and leading ones who called and reported to him all activities (failure to do so resulted in an offense). The trainees were even told that Philip was administrating the training. His power and position were growing immeasurably.

Statements made by some of the trainers in Taipei amazed us, as I am sure they did many others. Some examples are as follows:

1) "There is no need to pray about what to do; just follow the ministry."

2) We don't even need to think; we just do what we are told."

3) "Follow Witness Lee blindly. Even if he's wrong, he's right."

4) "If you leave the training, you'll miss the kingdom."

5) Our burden is to pick up Brother Lee's teaching and way to make us all Witness Lees, like a Witness Lee duplication center."

6) "To be one with the ministry is to be one with Brother Lee, the office, and Philip Lee."

7) Since Christianity is in ruins, the Lord raised up the recovery; since the recovery is in ruins, the Lord raised up the FTTT.

An account of Brother Lee's position was given by one of the leading trainers of the FTTT to a group of brothers in Dallas, Texas, in the summer of 1986, in the context of how to be one with the ministry. There are witnesses to confirm it. It goes as follows.

"The Father is number one, the Son is number two, the Spirit is number three, and Witness Lee is number four; and then there are those who are with Witness Lee." A brother asked, "And who is number five"? The trainer replied, "It is not yet quite clear who number five is", but pointing out "You brothers do not have access to brother Lee. I and another trainer do. We can walk into brother Lee's apartment any time and have breakfast with him. The way to know what brother Lee wants us to do is to be in contact with those who have access to him. They will tell you what he wants you to do." The hosting brother asked, "Isn't this a hierarchy?" The trainer replied, "No!" The brother asked, "How then does this differ from what we've been condemning?" The trainer answered, "If the elders in a local church would practice in this way to carry out their burden, it would be a hierarchy; but if this is practiced to carry out the ministry's burden, it is not a hierarchy."

When Brother Lee heard through us the above speech of his trainer, he took steps to rebuke and correct him. That such nonsense could be spoken by one chosen by Brother Lee to lead his training after all we have passed through and heard from Brother Lee's ministry is difficult to understand.

Many aspects of the training bothered us considerably. Elders who attended the training in Taipei were instructed explicitly to carry out the same training in their localities. Pressure was exerted upon the churches and elders to follow, implement, and conform to everything that came out in Taiwan. Failure to do so created problems. The effect on so much emphasis on ways, methods, and practices – all externals – resulted in a wilted wilderness condition among many of the saints.

Many faithful older saints were rebuked and given the impression that because of their age they were through. All official assertions to the contrary, the full-timers became a special class of people, and the full-time training was exalted above the churches, which were considered to have grown decrepit and were at best "better than nothing" (Andrew Yu, in Voice of the Young Heart). The elders were publicly degraded and blamed for all the ills. And yet the churches with the elders, and especially many of the older saints who were somewhat despised, gave generously and sacrificially to support the training. Their money was gladly accepted. In fact some of the churches were drained financially due to the heavy burden of supporting their full-timers and other projects that were promoted.

Video tapes of the FTTT convention on Nov. 23, 1986, and the FTTT graduation ceremony on June 1, 1987, surprised us with the mixture of worldly ways and gimmicks that were practiced and hitherto strongly condemned among us… I have no relish in mentioning these things. My object is to record and inform the readers of the matters that burdened and concerned us in the fall of 1987.

4. Misconduct Related to Personnel in the LSM Office

Last, but not least, there was the matter of serious misconduct related to the personnel in the LSM office. Our fear here is that this would eventually reach the ears of the media, and we would have a major public scandal to face. We remembered how in the latter days of the Exclusive Brethren in England there were extremely serious consequences due to various abuses which the saints could not cope with. This threatened us. Worst of all, the Lord's testimony would be smeared terribly, and Brother Lee's ministry would suffer great damage. These are the concerns that we wanted to share with Brother Lee.

MEETING WITH BROTHER LEE

December 12-16, 1987

On December 5th, 1987, Saturday, Brother Lee returned to Anaheim from Taiwan. Godfred Otuteye, Al Knoch and I plus a number of other brothers went to meet him at the Los Angeles Airport. As soon as time permitted, we called him at home and made an appointment to see him the following Saturday morning, December 12.

As the time drew near, we received a call from Ken Unger asking if he could accompany us on Saturday morning to see Brother Lee. He himself was intending to visit Brother Lee privately to express his concerns, but another brother in Orange County had counseled him not to go alone but to go with others. We agreed for Ken to come and we called Brother Lee. He also agreed.

Thus, on December 12, the four of us – Godfred, Al, Ken, and I – went to Brother Lee's home. We were thankful that we were finally having the opportunity to open our hearts to him. I began to speak with a few introductory remarks as follows: "Brother Lee, we have some deep concerns which we want to fellowship with you, concerns which in some ways make it difficult to know how to go on, as we will indicate. But as brothers and co-workers who have been very close to you for many years, we feel we owe it to you to speak our concerns in an honest and full way. We ask that you would please listen to us until the end and hold any remarks you may have until then. You may wonder why we are concerned about some points, but subsequent fellowship, we believe, will clear that up." We said this because we were afraid we would get hung up on some point and would not be able to present a full view of our concerns in the time we had. We, of course, would have been very happy to fellowship further concerning any matter if Brother Lee desired it, and we did indeed do that.

I continued then to share with him concerning the low state and morale of the churches, as we have mentioned before. I myself was aware of the condition of the churches in most area of the country. Concerning life, the level was very low; concerning truth, in some important aspects it was lacking and little apprehended; concerning service, there was very little heart to serve. Concerning the gospel, referring especially to Anaheim, though there were a few faithful ones caring for the new believers, the number had diminished considerably; moreover, the saints were polarized between those who go out and those who do not. I explained to him that it was not due to a lack of getting into the new move, since most elders and churches had done their utmost to carry out whatever his burden was.

Concerning Brother Lee's ministry, we had observed, appreciation for it had decreased, and to some extent the credibility of his ministry had been lowered. This was largely due to the fact that so many changes had been introduced and then retracted, and new change made, that many saints were pushed beyond their limit and could not tolerate anymore. We told Brother Lee that many brothers were concerned not only for the Lord's recovery, but for him and his ministry, which was a surely suffering.

I then spoke about what we felt at that time was one of the major causes of the deterioration, the excessive emphasis on numbers, methods, ways, and activities, which left many of the saints undernourished and dry. More seriously, I said that we had deviated from the central lane of God's economy according to Brother Lee's own words. I read to him what he had said about being distracted from life to increase in the publication entitled, "Practical Talks to the Elders" (quoted earlier). Then I analyzed briefly our history, pointing out that every time numbers were emphasized, serious problems were brought in and instead of an increase we eventually experienced a decrease. At a later date, when speaking to Brother Lee again about the excessive emphasis on increase, he replied, "Yes, I admit that whenever we touched the matter in the past we had problems, but we still need the increase." In years past we had a marvelous increase without emphasizing it at all.

I mentioned that by taking the way of seeking great numbers we were building the great tree of Matthew 13:31-32. Some of us will never forget Brother Lee's conference in 1963 in Los Angeles exposing the big tree of Matthew 13, referring to the church, which should by the proper growth of a mustard seed be like an herb, but which has grown abnormally great to become a tree, with its nature and function changed. He warned us strongly against this at that time.

I concluded by saying , "the Lord's recovery is in great jeopardy at this time. There is the great peril of emptiness and division, which we are already experiencing. If we did not speak to you, we would not be faithful to you or to the Lord. We need healing, we need relief, we need to be brought back to the enjoyment of Christ. Otherwise, the new way will not be successful and the saints will be incapable of receiving new help. We hope that maybe you, Brother Lee, may be able to help in this way, perhaps in the coming training."

Ken Unger continued and spoke with Brother Lee about the promotion and development of Philip Lee's influence. He mentioned how this promotion had begun in Irving, in 1981, under the leadership of Benson Phillips and Ray Graver. (Ken himself had been strongly influenced by them, and became in orange county one of the strongest proponents of the office and Philip Lee. This gave him an inside view of many things. His wife had faithfully served in the LSM office for years and also had seen and heard much. By this time Ken had deeply regretted his participation in this promotion.)

Ken then spoke of the influence of the LSM office over the churches. He reviewed the matters concerning this that we have outlined previously, and added this important point, that brothers were being frustrated from fellowshipping with Brother Lee directly. Rather they were told to fellowship with Philip Lee. We had passed through the very same kind of activity, only with another brother, in the crisis of 1977-1978.

Then Ken made a number of points of concern regarding the full-time training in Taipei. Some of these have also been outlined previously in this report. He referred to the arrogant attitude and the aberrational remarks of some of the trainers appointed by Brother Lee in Taipei which misrepresented Brother Lee's ministry. Ken himself had been one of the trainers in Taiwan, so he was familiar with many things. He pointed out how the FTTT was being viewed as a big organization having a hierarchy, with Philip Lee and the trainers at the top. One of the trainers had just recently (in the high school training in Irving, Texas) referred to some things that were being spoken in the "higher echelons of the Lord's recovery". Ken spoke strongly and frankly regarding his concerns for the Taipei training but at no time with Brother Lee did he or anyone else demand that the training be terminated.

Al Knoch then repeated to Brother Lee a number of statements made in the Taipei training and elsewhere that had stirred up our concern. Some of these have already been listed. Others that Al mentioned are as follows:

1. The prediction that the Lord is coming back in 13 years, setting a date for the Lord's return.

2. The talk of a global coordination, indicating that the elders and the churches should follow not only in principle, but also in detail, what comes out from Taipei. This global coordination was one of the goals of the gospel festival in Taipei in October 1987. There was also talk that the brothers in various places should keep in touch with Andrew Yu regularly to keep up with the latest details.

3. All the brothers must go to Taipei to be brought into the oneness they have there. If you have not gone to Taipei, you are not in the Lord's move.

4. A brother who was concerned for the saints in a certain church was told to forget the saints and go out, knock on doors, and raise up anew church life. Eventually some of the older saints would then join him.

5. Many people besides the Lord, in the FTTT, were elevated, flattered, called heroes, and publicly given awards. After Al had covered a fairly long list of statements, Brother Lee asked that the list be typed and a copy given to him. This was done, and we include a copy in the Appendix (see page 77, Appendix A). Al referred to all the worldliness

at the graduation ceremony in the stadium in Taiwan and then said, "Some of the saints have expressed the concern that the nature of the Lord's recovery is being changed."

Finally, Godfred spoke frankly and openly to Brother Lee concerning the serious misconduct related to personnel in the LSM office. Brother Lee listened attentively. I must say at this point that no time did Godfred or anyone else demand that the manager of the LSM office be discharged, as we are being accused of doing.

By this time, the morning had ended and we had to draw to a close. But we were most gratified by Brother Lee's response. He was very humble and receptive, beyond our anticipation, and he thanked us sincerely for our frankness and openness, shaking each one's hand. He begged us to pray with him and help him to handle the problem of the misconduct in the LSM office, regarding which he was especially concerned. We assured him that we would do what we could. He then urged us to return in the afternoon for further fellowship and prayer. We gladly consented, and left his home encouraged, yet still realizing it would be a difficult road ahead.

We returned to Brother Lee's home at 4:30 P. M. that afternoon at his request, expecting to have a good season of prayer. We urgently needed to pray. But we were disappointed when Brother Lee began, without prayer, to share with us for some time his burden for further steps in his work and ministry and the churches. Eventually we had some very brief prayer. Brother Lee then said that the hardest case to deal with was the misconduct in the LSM office. He asked us what we thought he should do, and we discussed the situation. Brother Lee remarked that all the things we shared with him in the morning regarding this matter may be true. Regarding the controlling of the churches by the management of the LSM Office, Brother Lee said that he had advised Philip Lee never to give any impression of such a thing. He told us that he had instructed him ten times never to touch the churches, the elders, the co-workers, or the work. That Brother Lee had to tell him ten times indicates that there was indeed a problem. But this matter, he said, would not be hard to deal with.

Brother Lee then requested that we return again in the evening for further fellowship, which we gladly agreed to. At 7:30 P. M. we met again and at the end of our talk, Brother Lee asked us to return again the following Monday morning. To this we also agreed. But when we left we were not so encouraged. Brother Lee, however, was quite concerned about finding a way to resolve the matter of the misconduct, realizing, I believe, that this was a substantial threat to his ministry.

Monday morning, December 14th, we came again to Brother Lee's home. After some brief prayer, Brother Lee gave his analysis of our past history, leading the very low rate of increase in recent years – in the U.S., in Taiwan, and in Germany. It was at this point that he admitted that the emphasis on increase in the past had brought trouble. He felt that we had a good start in the U.S., which reached a high point in 1969-70. Then we lost it. The migrations were the factor. In Los Angeles all the saints were concentrated in one place and under the proper leadership. But when the migrations came, what was gained in Los Angeles was lost. In 1974 he had the burden to put out the life-studies, and for twelve years he focused on that, neglecting the proper care of the churches. This also accounted for the loss and poor condition. The spread has been good, he said, but the increase has been short. No one rose up to care for the churches in Taiwan and the U. S. and he got disappointed. Where were the brothers, he asked, to care for the churches as in Elden Hall, Los Angeles?

He referred to the problem of the full-timers in Orange County. Who should care for them? To whom could he hand them over? The training from Taiwan had spread everywhere, he said. Only one church in the Far East was troubled by the training. The Lord got the victory in Taipei. But in the U.S., there were two groups of saints {those who agreed with him, and those who dissented from him}, which caused a real problem. England did not get much help, he stated, because they became opinionated, and opinions kill things. You must have one driver in the driver's seat. Where is the one accord today? Pooh! Brother Lee went on. At this juncture, he said, the problem of Philip Lee came in and made the clouds thicker. If the brothers were stronger, Philip Lee could never have come in. Benson Phillips' and Ray Graver's promotion of Philip Lee was wrong. Have I ever made Philip Lee a co-worker? He asked rhetorically. He remonstrated with the leading brothers among the Chinese saints, saying, why did you refer certain things to Philip Lee? Philip Lee is not ambitious, he said, but if you open to him and give him some ground, then he takes it.

Addressing us, Brother Lee asked, Why didn't you brothers with Bill Mallon come to me a long time ago with what was bothering you? (I have already said why we felt we needed to wait till Brother Lee returned from Taiwan in order to face to face.) Brother Lee then outlined his plans for the future. He said he would visit all the places and encourage the saints to enjoy Christ more and more. But by that alone the Lord would not be satisfied; we must go on to 1 Corinthians 14 {concerning the proper meetings}. We still need the old way, he said {perhaps by this he meant one-man ministry}, to bring them back and work on them. He himself must return to Taiwan, for they {the churches in Taiwan} were not yet steadily founded. He also had the burden to visit the churches in the U.S. and clear up many misunderstandings. I mention this talk of Brother Lee's in some detail to show what his thoughts were at that juncture.

A SURPRISING ELDERS' MEETING

December 14, 1987

On the evening of Monday, December 14, 1987, Brother Lee called a meeting of the elders of southern California. There was a fair number there representing most of the churches in the area. After prayer, Brother Lee opened the fellowship by giving a long word concerning the new way and its great success in Taiwan. Then he asked for fellowship from the brothers, desiring especially to know how successful the new way had been in their locality.

Dick Taylor, an elder in Long Beach, started with a lively, full-of enjoyment kind of testimony, such as Dick is well-known for, thanking the Lord for the door-knocking and the Gospel preaching in Long Beach, but ending with an honest word about the depression and the discouragement among some of the saints. This was unusual for Dick but he was telling it like it was. Other brothers followed who also spoke very honestly about dissensions concerning the new way and discouragement among the saints in their localities, for which they were very concerned. In some places divisions had arisen over the new way. John Smith, an elder in San Diego, ended the time of sharing with an honest account of his concerns for the saints in his church, mentioning how he feared that with the overemphasis on methods, numbers, and increase the saints would become activity-centered instead of Christ-centered.

What was extraordinary was the elders speaking up in such an honest and forthright way, knowing that such reports were not what Brother liked or wanted to hear. We were not accustomed to doing this due partly to a sense of intimidation. To my knowledge this was the first time that had been done. This was encouraging. But Brother Lee was visibly bothered, and later reacted strongly to the brothers' speaking, saying of one brother's sharing (John Smith's) that it was like pouring iced water on him. We were not the only ones who went to brother Lee with our concerns during these days. We heard that Dan Towle, individually, and Frank Scavo together with Dick Taylor also went to see Brother Lee to express to him their concerns about the present situation.

Brother Lee called the four of us who had met with him for another time of fellowship on Wednesday, December 16th, the day before he left for the winter training in Irving. The fellowship did not issue in any conclusions. He said then that he wanted to continue to meet with us after he returned from the training to resolve the problem related to the LSM office. We agreed.

Ken Unger and I were burdened to attend the coming elders' meetings to take place prior to the winter training in Irving, Texas, December 22 and 23, 1987. We prepared to leave on December 19th, a few days early, as we desired to have an opportunity to speak with Benson Phillips and Ray Graver before the elders' meetings commenced.

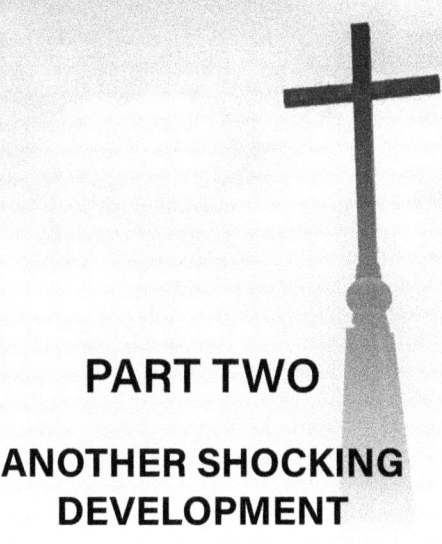

PART TWO

ANOTHER SHOCKING DEVELOPMENT

December 19,1987

In the morning of December 19, just before Ken and I were to leave for Texas that afternoon, the sister from the LSM office who had spoken to me on September 30th (see page 10) called and asked to speak to Godfred and me. We met with her and were utterly amazed at what we heard. He began to relate to us in detail some of the things she suffered while in the service of the LSM office. She wanted us to realize how grave the problem was. We were revulsed to the depths of our being, and when the conversation ended and we parted, we we're so full of abhorrent feelings that we were literally in a daze.

Godfred drove me to the airport to meet Ken. We were in a state of shock and utter disgust. All this had taken place in what we called the Lord's recovery! We felt that Benson Phillips and Ray Graver, who were deeply involved in the LSM operation, must surely know something about these matters. Therefore, we resolved to confer with them about this when we got to Irving.

ELDERS' MEETINGS AND FELLOWSHIP WITH BROTHERS IN IRVING, TEXAS

December 1987

On Saturday afternoon, December 19th Ken Unger and I flew to Irving. I did not relate to him what the sister from the LSM office had just told us. On Monday, December 21st, we made an appointment to see Benson Phillips and Ray Graver in the morning. Having been intimate co-workers with them for many years, and knowing that they were aware of many things, we mentioned the concerns that we had presented to Brother Lee on December 12th, excluding the matter of the misconduct in the LSM office. We wanted especially to let them know how strongly we felt regarding the colossal mistake they had made in promoting and exalting the office and Philip Lee, starting in 1981. They said that they did not feel they had erred much. This really surprised and disappointed us. We tried to impress them how serious this matter was. They invited us out for dinner, and we decided to meet again in the afternoon to continue our fellowship.

Upon coming together, we attempted amid protests to mention the matter of the misconduct in the LSM office. They steadfastly refused to hear about it, but we proceeded to speak. Ray Graver then quickly rose and exited the room. Benson (in whose home we were meeting) also rose to register his displeasure. We felt that they had knowledge relevant to the matter and wanted to confer with them about it. Benson admitted that the same sister from the LSM office (mentioned previously) had come to him in Taipei to disclose a related event, but he strongly protested our bringing this matter before them. They argued that this affair was exclusively under the jurisdiction of the church in Anaheim, and they had no business being involved. We felt, as we mentioned earlier, that it was more than local, and that since that they were leaders in the LSM operation, they could be consulted. Some time later, however, I apologized to Benson and Ray for this, feeling that if they chose not to hear, we should not have forced the issue.

That night we met with some of the elders who had arrived for the elders' meetings and had some fellowship and prayer. At the same time Bill Mallon was meeting with Brother Lee to open his heart to him. The next morning, December 22nd, the elders' meetings began with Brother Lee giving a word that was well accepted. While speaking, he referred to Bill Mallon with very commendatory words, saying that he wanted all the brothers to know that he stood with Bill, and he was not happy that other brothers had criticized Bill. Titus Chu, seeking to encourage Bill, said that Brother Lee had never done that for any brother. I personally had never heard Brother Lee support a brother so strongly.

In the elders' meeting that night the atmosphere entirely changed. Brother Lee was fighting mad. It seemed clear to us that Benson Phillips and Ray Graver had gone to Brother Lee that afternoon and told him all that we had told them. He was on fire. His whole message was a vindication of himself regarding some of the concerns we had shared with him. It was obvious that he was rebuking and dealing with us publicly, though not mentioning our names. We had seen him do this kind of thing a number of times with other brothers. Perhaps he feels that this is the scriptural way.

The next morning in the last elders' meeting, Brother Lee went at it again, lashing out fiercely concerning a number of things. He was exceedingly hot and strongly vindicated himself while rebuking his supposed opposers, especially us. I felt he was not fair, not speaking truly, and not acting appropriately. A number of brothers were grieved and disturbed. After the meeting I went up to him and asked if we could have a little time of fellowship that afternoon. He was quite willing and we set the time at 3:30 P.M.

Following my contact with Brother Lee after the meeting, John Chang, one of the leaders in Orange County among the Chinese saints, approached Ken and me. Ken had talked at length with John the previous evening and discovered that he shared many of the same concerns we did. This brother in the morning meeting had sat next to one of the leading elders from Taipei, Lin Rong, and had mentioned to him that we were very concerned about the present situation. Lin Rong responded that he would like to have some time with Ken and me if we were willing and if it could be arranged. John Chang told us about this, and we consented to meet with him, agreeing to have lunch together. This we did – Lin Rong, John Chang, Ken Unger, and myself. We were really surprised that one of the elders from Taipei would like to speak to us and that he too was concerned, and we wondered what would come out of that.

At the restaurant we began to fellowship. Lin Rong appeared very solicitous of the fellowship and indicated that he also was quite concerned about the situation, although I noted that he never mentioned what his concerns were. He was desirous to know our concerns, so we opened to him and eventually mentioned, with tears, the items we had shared with Brother Lee. He listened attentively. We then left, delivering the brothers to their respective dwellings, and asking Lin Rong to keep what we had shared with him in confidence. He said he would.

That afternoon I went to Brother Lee's apartment according to our appointment. My desire was to assure him that I was not opposing his burden as set forth in the main points of the "new way" (as it was defined in those days). He had indicated that we were indeed opposing. I told him that I was absolutely not against the preaching of the gospel by door-knocking or by any way; that I was absolutely not against the practice of home meetings; and that I was not against any other matter he emphasized. Rather, I was for these things. Brother Lee received my fellowship and remarked that he had never had any problem with me; he only felt that I should have stayed in Anaheim more and not traveled so much. Our talk ended peacefully, but I was not encouraged.

That evening the winter training began, and the next morning Ken and I together with Dick Taylor caught an early flight back to Los Angeles. At the airport to meet us, according to an arrangement made in Irving, was Gene Gruhler. Gene wanted, he said, to have a time of fellowship with me, and the only time available was to talk as we drove back to Anaheim from the airport. The conversation in the car was not pleasant. I rebuked Gene, and he rebuked me. I rebuked him for something he said in the elders' meetings in Irving which I felt misrepresented the feeling of a number of. He rebuked me for sharing my concerns with others, which he felt was forming a party. Actually, I had only spoken to a few brothers at that time, brothers with whom I was closely related in the Lord's work and with whom I had opened my heart for years. And, it was for the purpose of going to see Brother Lee together. I did not consider this forming a party.)

Then Gene said that if we didn't take Brother Lee's leadership, who would be the leader? "You??!!" he said, indicating me. But I had no desire to be such a leader; I am not that kind of person. He exhorted me to take Brother Lee's leadership. I told Gene that I would follow Brother Lee's leadership in the sphere of life and truth. Gene interpreted that to mean that I would not follow his leadership in practice, and he remonstrated with me concerning this. In some things that was true. I could not conscientiously follow everything in all good faith as I had done before. Gene's intention, no doubt, was to try to help me, and I appreciate that. He surely was disappointed. He dropped Ken and me off at my house and then went to see Al Knoch to try to render him some help. So ended a turbulent and exhausting trip to Texas.

FURTHER MEETING WITH
BROTHER LEE

January 30, 1988

After Brother Lee returned from the training in Irving, he called me on the phone and said that he would like to meet with Ken Unger and me on Thursday night, January 7th, 1988, and with Al Knoch, Godfred Otuteye, Ken Unger, and me on Friday night, January 8th.

On Thursday evening, Ken and I sat before Brother Lee in his home. He told us at the outset that he knew about our talk with Benson and Ray and what we said to them (we were already aware of that). He also told us that he knew about our meeting with Lin Rong, the Taipei elder. Lin Rong had gone to Brother Lee, and, we believe, to others following our time with him and informed them of everything we said. This is the one who had come to us apparently so solicitous and with all confidentiality. It is not that we were ashamed of what we said, but his motive in seeking our fellowship was highly suspect and his conduct unethical and reprehensible. I was disgusted.

Brother Lee was very disturbed by some of the things we said to these brothers. He heard that in speaking to Lin Rong we made reference to "central control" among the churches, and this was a very great offense to him. I told Brother Lee that what we actually said was that there was a tendency toward centralization. Central control and centralization, of course, indicate approximately the same thing, though the term centralization puts the practice in a little better light, reducing somewhat the idea of control. In retrospect, we had much more than a tendency toward centralization. This word went to the heart of the problem. We always had said that our headquarters was not in Anaheim or in Taipei or in any place on this earth, but in the heavens. Could we honestly say that now? Taipei was called the center of the universe by some in the full-time training in Taiwan.

Brother Lee mentioned then that Bill Mallon, John So, and myself all used the same term – central control. He deduced that we must have consulted or "conspired" together. The fact was that we all had the same realization because of separate similar experiences without any consultation and certainly without any "conspiring " with each other. John So began to be concerned in 1986, Bill Mallon in the spring of 1987, and myself in the fall of 1987. Eventually, as we had done for years, we had telephone contact with each other, and our heart's burden came out.

The next evening, Friday, January 8th, the four of us met again with Brother Lee at his request. – Al, Godfred, Ken, and I. He condemned us strongly for the way we had handled things and said that we were no longer qualified to help him deal with the misconduct in the LSM office or to deal with it as the church. He was especially perturbed that we had brought up this matter with Benson and Ray and also with Lin Rong. Thus, he said we had disqualified ourselves. Brother Lee's attitude and demeanor were very disturbing to us. Outside his home, after we left, we conversed for a few minutes, all of us somewhat in a daze, deeply disappointed and troubled. There was a hardness in our brother that made us feel it was hopeless to engage in any further fellowship.

BROTHER LEE MEETS WITH
THE FULL-TIMERS AND ELDERS

January 30, 1988

On Saturday morning, January 30th, Brother Lee met with all the full-timers in Orange County, along with a number of the elders. He gave them a message and then took them all out from under the hand of the LSM office and turned them over to the churches, charging them to submit to the elders in the localities in Orange County where they lived and served. They were divided among the churches in Anaheim, Fullerton, Huntington Beach, Irvine, Cypress, and Long Beach. We all felt that this was a positive move on behalf of the full-timers, putting them in a more normal situation in the sphere of the church life. Brother Lee expected that the elders in each locality would assist and direct them I their service and study of the Word.

In Anaheim there were about twelve full-timers or part-timers for whom we were responsible. They were indeed precious and prospective young people. I always considered them such and never said anything to the contrary, as I am being charged. We loved them and cared for them. (I am still in contact and good fellowship with a number of them.) We were burdened to help them get into the Word regularly and diligently; hence for four mornings every week beginning in February 1988 Al Knoch and I labored with them in the Word, beginning in Philippians, then Galatians, and then Colossians. This brought us into the month of June, when we stopped in time for the summer training. The word was very rich to us and full of light.

A few of the full-timers began to acquire jobs, and after the summer training others felt that they also needed employment to care for the living expenses. The church in Anaheim did its best to help support some of them, but one couple felt in their conscience that the fruit of their work did not merit the support, and they preferred to earn a living themselves. Some, incidentally, were very disappointed with the progress of the new ones from whom they were caring, especially one couple who were doing their best to care for a few Spanish-speaking people baptized during the "blitz." By the summer months there was hardly anyone left who could serve on a full-time basis. And so passed another stage. It was not a totally normal situation either for the full-timers or for the church.

A VERY THREATENING INCIDENT

December 1987 – March 1988

In late December a brother in the church in Anaheim who had been severely damaged through the misconduct in LSM office was so traumatized psychologically that he sought revenge and took definite steps to execute a very grave act. (Thank God it never happened.) This came to the ears of one of the elders in Anaheim, who without any delay met with him to calm and divert him. Some time later, two of us met with him. The dear brother was greatly disturbed emotionally, with good cause humanly speaking. But, he was very open to us, and the Lord was merciful to him. Actually, he had already halted in his course – the Lord would not let him proceed – but his feelings were still very raw, and he desperately needed help. We loved him and did our best to comfort him. This incident illustrates the gravity of the situation.

In March 1988 this affair also came to the ears of Dan Towle, who was an elder in Fullerton, and who with great alarm took upon himself to call Brother Lee and divulge all the details to him. He did not know that the brothers in Anaheim were already caring for the brother, since he did not take pains to call them. Brother Lee told him to contact us. So he called, telling us what he had done and asking for fellowship. We got together – Dan, Godfred, and I. We were very annoyed with Dan for taking matters into his own hands and calling brother Lee without contacting the brothers in Anaheim and we told him so. The course he had taken totally neglected the proper fellowship among the churches we should have. Of course, he was relieved to hear that the problem was resolved.

SPECIAL FELLOWSHIP WITH BROTHER LEE

March 24, 26, 1988

There was a couple in Anaheim who were seriously injured by the misconduct related to the LSM office, and they were deeply offended with Brother Lee for tolerating such a situation to exist and also for not giving them an ear to relate the problems they had experienced when they went to him earlier in the year. We felt that Brother Lee should be made aware of the great offense on his part suffered by this couple, therefore we requested a time to speak with him. It was granted and on March 24, Godfred, Al, and I met with Brother Lee in his home. We explained the feeling of the couple toward him and appealed to him to give them a hearing. He agreed to do this, and a date was set for the following Saturday.

While we were with Brother Lee, he remarked that it had been one hundred days since we had come to him on December 12th 1987, and opened our hearts regarding our concerns. He said that not one day had passed that he did not consider what to do. Moreover, he added that he felt that he should not do anything and not succumb to any pressure exercised upon him.

On Saturday evening, March 26th, Godfred, myself, and the husband of this couple met with Brother Lee. (Brother Lee felt it would be too awkward for the wife to be there as well.) The husband opened up with a very good attitude and related in some detail the mistreatment his wife had experienced in serving with the LSM office in the full-time training in Taipei. Brother Lee listened attentively with a most serious demeanor, and then expressed his feeling of sorrow for the whole affair, saying, "My heart is broken!" He explained why he did not feel free to listen to them previously, and then spoke of his appreciation for the faithful service of the wife over many years. At the end of the time Brother Lee pronounced the Lord's blessing on this brother and his wife. We prayed and then departed, the brother feeling somewhat relieved that he was able to discharge his grief and burden to Brother Lee, but still not at all happy about the whole affair. This was the settlement rendered on one side to deal with a very serious offense stemming from the service in the LSM office.

CONFERENCES IN CHARLOTTE AND MIAMI

April 1988

On Easter weekend, April 1-3, 1988, the church in Charlotte, N. C. invited me to come and share the word of the Lord. I did so. Many saints representing the churches in North and South Carolina plus some from Virginia and Georgia gathered for the conference. I ministered to them concerning the Lord's word to the seven churches in Revelation 2 and 3, mentioning nothing whatever of the problems we had encountered. We emphasized the need of coming back to the beginning, as the Apostle John emphasized in his ministry, back to Christ as the tree of life and back to our first love for Him.

A number of brothers in North Carolina – in Charlotte, Greensboro, Chapel Hill, and Raleigh – already had very much the same concerns as we had, and we fellowshipped with them outside the conference meetings regarding our situation in the work, the ministry office, and the churches. We also talked with Brother John Little, who came there from Nashville, about some of the present problems, and he was very open to us, agreeing at that time with all our concerns regarding the present situation in the work, the ministry office, and the churches. We were burdened to open to him since we had known him well for many years and wanted him to know how we felt.

At the end of April 1988, I was invited to come to Miami, Florida, for a conference with the churches in Southern Florida. It was held April 29th through May 1st. I spoke there again on the Lord's word to the seven churches, but in a different way, this time emphasizing the practicality and spirituality of the local churches: the practicality being embodied in the local nature of the church, and the spirituality in the three matters of love, life, and light, so stressed in John's ministry. Concerning the practicality, I emphasized the need for local administration in every church balanced with mutual fellowship together among all the churches. I had been helped much through a re-reading of Brother Watchman Nee's The Normal Christian Church Life to see the "intensely local" nature of the church and as a result felt that we were seriously straying from this important aspect. I stressed in the conference the need for the elders in each church to go directly to the Lord praying and seeking His leading regarding their particular church, just as the parents of a family take special care for the needs of their own family, whatever the requirements of other families might be. This preserves the practical, real, and direct headship of Christ over His people. On the other hand, there is the need for much fellowship universally with other churches and all saints to receive their grace, their fellowship, their portion, walking together with them as one body. This preserves the reality and organic unity of the Body of Christ. We need both the local administration and universal mutual fellowship. This was my main burden.

After the conference I had several times of fellowship with a smaller group of brothers with whom I shared some of our concerns regarding the present situation in the churches. I sincerely regretted after these times of smaller group fellowship that we dwelt too much on the problems and not adequately on the positive side of our going on. The content of our fellowship, however, did express my honest observations and concerns.

Brother Lee informed me at a later date that a full report of what I had spoken both publicly in the large meetings and privately in the smaller groups was passed on to him. Some of the things I was reported to have said troubled him and offended him greatly, and he has repeated them many times. Perhaps I should address and give a true account of some of the matters at this juncture.

In the last meeting of the conference, I made reference to Abraham's marriage to Hagar and its fruit, Ishmael. However, I made no application to our present situation, as the tape recordings of that meeting will bear out. We had been studying Galatians with the full-timers in Anaheim, and the passage concerning Abraham and Hagar in chapter four had been freshly and deeply impressed upon me. In the small group meetings, I made some remarks that I felt we were indeed in danger in the present move of participating in the works of the flesh as Abraham did with Hagar with the result of bringing forth Ishmael. We also noted that because of this act God did not appear to Abraham for thirteen years. It has been reported that I said these thirteen years, in our present experience, started from 1974 (when Brother Lee began the Life Studies of the Bible) and continued to 1987. This surprised me. I do not remember ever having this thought, to say nothing about speaking it. Moreover, I do not believe that the Lord did not speak to us during that period. Much was being said in Taipei about their being thirteen years until the Lord comes back, from 1987 till 2000. Now that particular thirteen years did occur to me as having a possibility of similarity, and I feared that what happened to Abraham might be our plight in the coming years. I believe I mentioned this to the brothers at that time. Perhaps this is what the reporter was referring to.

The conference in Miami caused a great stir, particularly regarding our comments on the local administration of the churches. This was the first time I had ever spoken this, and it came out of a fresh realization and burden, though it was a truth I always believed to be scriptural. I will refer to this matter later in the narrative.

AN UNPRECEDENTED MEETING IN ANAHEIM

May 15, 1988

It had been our habit in the church life for the elders to make all the decisions concerning meetings, service, etc., and simply announce them to the saints, expecting everyone to comply and follow, which most did. What we greatly lacked was adequate fellowship with the saints to learn their feeling regarding various aspects of the church life. We were impressed that we should proceed no longer with this glaring deficiency of communication, nor should we make all the decisions by ourselves and hand them down as a kind of ruling oligarchy.

In the church in Anaheim during the Spring of 1988 it was necessary to come to some conclusions regarding the schedule of our meetings and the place of the Lord's Table meeting, whether in the homes or in the hall. We believed that it was fitting to call a special meeting of all the saints to seek the best way together. This we did on the Lord's Day evening, May 15th. The atmosphere was excellent, and everyone was very happy and participated well. Many shared their impression concerning the issues, and the decisions were made in a very good flow with the whole body concurring. The saints felt honored and appreciative that they were all included and could participate as proper members of the Body. After the meeting we had a love feast, and one brother said to me exultingly, "Hallelujah, I'm actually a member of the Body!"

For this organic function of the Body to succeed, it is imperative, of course, to be in the Spirit, denying themselves, and open to the Lord and to one another. The saints should be encouraged to do this. Although there may be difficulties, with patience and faith and the flesh being brought into subjection, I believe we will have a further experience of the fellowship of the Body. We do not mean by this to practice a democracy. We are not for that. Neither are we for a theocracy or an oligarchy. We desire a true theocracy, the kingdom of God, where the Head makes His mind known through the members of His Body.

PART THREE

SOME ANAHEIM SAINTS HEAR OF SERIOUS PROBLEMS

Spring, Summer 1988

During the Spring of 1988 some of the Anaheim saints began to hear, not through us but others, the serious improprieties in the LSM office, and they were infuriated. We had endeavored to cover such matters, hoping there could be a satisfactory resolution to the problems without disturbing the saints, but it was of no avail. Others who knew or found out thought that it should be exposed. Word spread fast, and by the summer months the number of saints who were affected swelled considerably. Some had been personally mistreated by the LSM office and were very indignant and bitter. Some who could not cope with the reports that came to them refused to hear anything at all, calling everything a pack of lies. We were very grieved about the whole situation and hardly knew what to do.

On Saturday evening, August 6th, Godfred and I met with thirty-four saints, at their invitation, in a sister's home. Most of them had already withdrawn from the church meetings and were in a state of great disgust and revulsion with the Living Stream Ministry, with Brother Lee, and with the church for any supposed relationship with the LSM and Brother Lee. We listened while they poured out their complaints and vented their abhorrence of what they had seen and heard. Most of them had given a good part of their lives to what they considered to be the Lord's recovery, and they felt deeply cheated and violated.

Word was passed around that the elders were coming to that meeting, and they welcomed the opportunity to confront us and urge us to action. They urgently demanded that we make a public announcement in the church meetings, completely severing and disassociating ourselves from the Living Stream Ministry. We addressed them finally expressing our concern for the situation, yet maintaining that we must have the clear leading and support of the Lord before making any public stand. Most of them could not hide their disappointment with us, and could not understand why we would not speak out immediately to deal with unrighteousness, throwing caution to the wind. We were endeavoring to care for everything and everyone involved in a proper way.

The following Wednesday evening, August 10th, Godfred and I joined by John So (who had recently come to Anaheim with his family), met with these saints, thirty-four in number. They all looked to John So for counsel, and he gave them a very wise word to fit the situation, saying that the elders should move positively to render solid ministry to the church, bringing the saints back to Christ. He urged all in that gathering to come to the church meetings to support the elders. What they had done in Germany to deal with the problem, he said, could not be done in Anaheim, and they should not expect that since here is a divided situation. A number of them were very disappointed with John since he did not advocate a strong course of reaction. One brother there, asked John if a real apostle could become a false apostle. John replied that he honestly did not know; he had never thought about it. The next morning John So left to return to Europe.

Following these meetings Godfred, Al, and I had serious fellowship regarding how to face the situation. These thirty-four saints represented a significant portion of the church. We knew we had to try to help them as well as all the others. Hence, we felt that we needed a meeting to make our standing as the church clear to everyone on both sides, whether for or against a relationship with the LSM, so that all may be helped to see where they should stand and how we should go on. Therefore, a special meeting for the whole church was announced for the Lord's Day evening, August 28th.

Meanwhile Brother Lee was visiting churches in the Northwest, speaking out against "autonomy" and "federation." Saints in the Northwest came together in Seattle over the weekend of August 19-21. We heard that brothers were stirred up to fight against the "winds of teaching" (like autonomy) being brought into the Lord's recovery.

FELLOWSHIP WITH THE ELDERS IN THE ANAHEIM CHINESE-SPEAKING MEETINGS

August 18, 1988

In the Spring of 1988, Minoru Chen had returned from his stay in Taiwan as a trainer in the FTTT to resume his eldership in Anaheim, as appointed by Brother Lee in February 1986. Yet for some months he had hardly any contact with us. On Thursday evening, August 18th, Godfred and I had a long and frank fellowship with him. Godfred spoke at length, presenting his realization of the misconduct in the LSM office. I gave an account of my realization of the whole situation and our present standing. Minoru listened passively to our fellowship. Due to the lateness of the hour, he was unable to reply adequately. We had confronted Minoru with reports that he had spoken negatively about us behind our backs to others about grave concerns he had for us, his fellow elders. He admitted that he had done this to the leading brothers in the Chinese-speaking work.

On Friday evening, August 26th Godfred, Al, and I came together with Philip Lin and Minoru Chen, the two elders on the Chinese-speaking side. Altogether we constituted the five elders of the church in Anaheim. We noted that this was the first time ever that all five of us had come together for fellowship. That was remarkable, since we had all been in the position of elders since February 1986, two and one half years prior to that time. We had some very frank fellowship regarding the problem of the Chinese-speaking meetings, which had always been a source of great frustration and troubling to the church since they were started in 1980. It was as if we had two different churches in Anaheim with two different leadings, a situation that we simply tolerated and could do very little about because of the involvement of Brother Lee and the Living Stream Ministry with the Chinese-speaking meetings. The brothers insisted that they considered the Chinese-speaking meetings a part of the church, and they desired henceforth to practice that oneness under one eldership. This began a period in which we sought to maintain more fellowship and coordination as one eldership with these brothers. Minoru inquired regarding the content of the special meeting set for August 28th, and Godfred gave him a resume of the points we would cover.

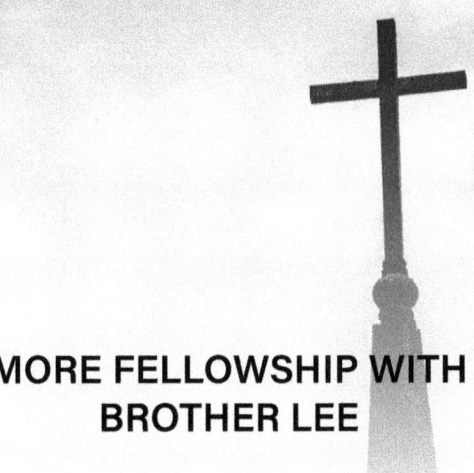

MORE FELLOWSHIP WITH
BROTHER LEE

August 25, 26, 1988

On Thursday, August 25th, Brother Lee asked me to come to his home for further fellowship. He said then that he would ask Godfred and Al to come to his home the following day, Friday. It seemed strange to me that he would separate us, asking me to come on one day and them on another. But he said I could come too on Friday if I liked. On Thursday alone with me, Brother Lee asked me what changes I thought he should have. This greatly surprised me. Perhaps he was thinking of my fellowship with him on June 22nd, when I told him that if he did not have some change, it would be difficult for the churches to go on. I said, "Brother Lee, please give me a moment to collect my thoughts." I was concerned about what I should say to him. Then I proceeded to mention a few of the concerns previously mentioned. Moreover, I tried to impress him that I never tried to use the term "autonomy" in all of my speaking. Throughout these months I had told him this several times. I stated that I was burdened to speak about local administration together with universal fellowship (as we have in our hymn, #824, authored by Brother Lee and translated from Chinese: Administration local, each answering to the Lord; Communion universal, upheld in one accord.) He responded, "That's my teaching." I agreed that it was indeed his teaching. So, what was wrong?

The next afternoon, Friday, August 26th, I joined Godfred and Al at Brother Lee's home. Godfred spoke strongly, asking Brother Lee first if he had spoken anything against us recently. He replied that he had not. Then Godfred reasoned with him: How is it that you speak against autonomy, considering that a problem, but you will not deal with the problems that we brought to your attention. Godfred spoke earnestly and impressively. He said, "the center of the church should be Christ, but He has been replaced by you and your ministry." Brother Lee was touched by what Godfred said, and perhaps considering that what he had just alleged afforded some light for clearing up the problem, he said, "I like to hear that." I recall the scene vividly, and his words still echo in my ears. It seemed that this time Brother Lee appreciated the frank fellowship and was trying to warm up to us. But we could not seem to make any real progress. Brother Lee remarked that everything that had happened in Europe which had caused so great a problem between the churches and the Living Stream Ministry was just a misunderstanding. After the meeting Godfred told us that he wanted to leave the eldership and was fully disgusted with the whole situation.

SIXTEEN POINTS

August 28, 1988

As the day drew near for special fellowship with the church as we had announced, Godfred, Al and I came together for prayer and fellowship regarding the content of the coming gathering. We only knew that we needed to clear up some matters, and set a direction for the church, and we had been praying individually for guidance concerning the specific points that should be covered. I proposed to the brothers that we briefly expound a number of basic matters according to the Word of God that set forth the proper standing of the church, touching especially the aspects both of truth and practice that related to our current situation. The brothers consented. After some consideration we decided that I would cover eight points concerning the truth and Godfred would cover eight points regarding the practice; in conclusion Al would give a testimony of confirmation.

The appointed time arrived for the meeting. (Brother Lee meanwhile was in San Gabriel, meeting with the Chinese-speaking saints.) This time, we felt, was very crucial to our going on. There were over two hundred saints on hand, including some on the Chinese-speaking side who understood English (a good number considering our usual attendance). Brothers Minoru Chen and Philip Lin with the three of us sat together in the front. We launched into our burden and experienced much strengthening, release, and anointing. As contemplated, I covered the points concerning our standing related to the truth. This touched the following points (in a greatly abridged form):

1. Our standing in relation to the Word of God. It is our sole authority, our constitution, and we should check everything by it.

2. Our standing concerning the church. In this age the church is central and supreme; no other corporate body is recognized by the New Testament.

3. Concerning the genuine oneness. It is organic; it can never be organized or forced. Spiritual leaders should not divide us.

4. Concerning other Christians. We should never mock or belittle other Christians with an elitist attitude; rather, we should love, honor, and receive them all.

5. Concerning our vocation. It is to build up the Body of Christ, not any work or ministry.

6. Concerning our purpose or aim. It is to be the Lord's testimony; we are not here for any work.

7. Concerning the ministry. It is the imparting of God into His people to produce the church. It is not the ministry of any one person; we all have a share in it.

8. Concerning the apostles. They are always plural, and there are a number of them on the earth today. We should not exalt any apostle or servant of God beyond what is written.

The full text of my points as well as Godfred's plus Al's testimony is included in the Appendix (see page 79, Appendix B).

I spoke honestly and frankly according to the solid principles revealed in the Word, which we had been taught and which we had believed and held for years, applying some of the points to our present situation. I was not aiming at Brother Lee. I was burdened to present the basic truths concerning our standing and correct some misconceptions held by the saints. The present need demanded that we touch specifically the matters which we addressed. I have heard Brother Lee repeat a number of times what he had been told by a brother. "These sixteen points are sixteen bullets aimed at you {Brother Lee}." That is not true. If anything hit him it is not because we were aiming at him.

Godfred followed and covered eight points regarding our practice:

1. In relation to church administration. It should be local, with no central control. The elders in each place should seek the Lord directly for his timely leading according to the need in their locality.

2. The Living Stream Ministry Office. It is a business office and has no authority over the church. As the church we disassociate ourselves from certain practices and conduct there that we find intolerable.

3. The Life Studies and Christian literature in general. We should never allow spiritual materials to become a crutch or replacement for the reading of the Bible. To insist upon reading only LSM material or to oppose the reading of LSM material is going to far.

4. The church book sales. We will continue this service, but we will no longer advertise or promote any books.

5. The semi-annual trainings. We will no longer interrupt our church life for the trainings. Anyone who wishes to attend the trainings should feel free to do so.

6. The other churches. We should respect and highly esteem all other churches, but we should not compel the church in our locality to practice like other churches.

7. Various practices. In all these matters we must practice generality. Any practice which is not sinful we should not oppose; neither should we impose it.

8. The gospel. There is no particular way to preach the gospel; any proper way is good.

Godfred spoke earnestly and to the point with a good spirit. He apologized to the church on our behalf for coming under the influence of external pressures in past years and not seeking the Lord's leading directly according to the local need. He confessed to the saints on our behalf the promoting of an improper relationship with the LSM office, so that we declared our oneness with that office and thus associated ourselves with its conduct. The blame for that relationship, he said, must be borne by us elders, and not put on the doorstep of the office.

Godfred closed with this statement, which I want to quote in full: "Our reason for having this fellowship is not to vindicate anyone or to condemn anyone, or to do anything for ourselves. We are having this fellowship for the purpose of bringing us all back to the Lord Himself. He is our Head, He is our center; and He should be the entire unique content of the church life! We hope that the things we have briefly mentioned will clear up the past so that we all can go forward together positively as the church in our city." This was a fitting conclusion to the sixteen points.

Al Knoch then followed with an appropriate confirming testimony, saying that we were not there to oppose anything which the Lord had given us through the years. He cited questions being raised by saints in local churches in Europe, where he had recently visited with his family. They were asking, "Are we really the local church with a general standing, open to every Christian in our city? Or are we a sect?" These are legitimate and timely questions. Then he added, "They found out that gradually they were becoming a very special kind of 'church', not a local church...." Al also apologized for his part in all the promotions and for all that he had done and said.

When Al finished, I spoke just a few words regarding our going on, how we needed much prayer and the Word. We did not have time to impress these matters upon the saints, so we just made a few announcements, expecting that the meeting would soon be brought to a close.

When I sat down a number of brothers, most of whom were in the home meetings Godfred and I visited a few weeks previously (see pages 37 and 38), were very burdened to speak and had come to the meeting well-prepared. They felt that what we had spoken had left the job only half done, and they desired to complete it. Therefore, they stood one by one crying out against various evils and especially remonstrating against sin being tolerated and sinful people being put into a position of influence. One brother quoted Watchman Nee's word that the judgment of sin is the basis of oneness. (Love One Another, pp. 148-149). The pent-up feelings of some of them burst out in strong protest against practices and abuses they could brook no longer. Although we sympathized with a number of their burdens, we felt the spirit of the meeting had changed, and there was considerable stridency and rancor. That left a bad taste. Accusations were made and some personal matters were raised that should have been handled in private, not in that forum. The meeting began to erupt in an exchange of words at the end, and Godfred arose and with God-given wisdom calmed the storm and turned the saints to pray. Thus, concluding the meeting. We regretted that it should end in such a manner.

Toward the conclusion of the session as we were starting to pray, Minoru arose and made a couple of statements which I want to note for the record. He said that he agreed in principle with all the points that we had made, but he stated that he wanted to reserve himself regarding some matters; and concerning some of the points, particularly those made by Godfred, he stated that he would not say in a definite way that he agreed or disagreed. He also referred to Godfred's apology for participating in certain promotions, which, he said, took place mainly in 1986. (He was alluding to the promotion of the LSM office and Philip Lee.) He said that he wanted to amen what Godfred had shared and declared that there was an excessive amount of this promotion, thereby bringing the saints into confusion and despondency, and the church into suffering. He also wanted to ask the forgiveness of the whole church for his part in this very matter.

Some are saying today that our presentation of the sixteen points concerning our standing opened the door for all the other speaking that began that night and continued for many weeks. This is definitely not true. Those who spoke at the end of the meeting on August 28th, together with others who did not speak, were at the bursting point, somewhat similar to the oppressed people of Eastern Europe in recent times. They came prepared to occupy as much time as would be given to them. One of them said that he came with a notebook full of material to present. Hence what we spoke, or whether we spoke at all, made little difference.

The meeting was finally dismissed at a late hour, and I retired to my home and rested that night filled with a profound peace that what we had spoken in the sixteen points was right and was delivered in a proper spirit. I only regretted that the meeting could not have been concluded in a better way, and that the last part diluted the impact of the first.

A few weeks later we discovered that the sixteen points Godfred and I shared together with Al's confirming testimony had been transcribed, edited, and printed, and were being mailed out all over the world – all this without our knowledge. Belatedly I was able to obtain a copy and perused it, finding it, happily, to be an accurate and well-edited rendering of the spoken form. We had no prior thought or intention whatever that the contents of that meeting would be disseminated. We considered the meeting and the points to be totally a local affair. But this distribution was out of our hands, and by that time, had we desired, there was nothing we could do about it. However, I believe it was sovereignly allowed of the Lord.

FURTHER FELLOWSHIP WITH
BENSON PHILLIPS

September 12, 1988

On September 10th, Benson Phillips, who had been in Anaheim for several days caring for LSM affairs, called me and asked for a time of fellowship. We made an appointment for Monday evening, September 12th. Al Knoch joined us that evening. Benson declared that he wanted to keep the oneness with us, not allowing anything to come between us and separate us. We appreciated that. We spoke with him further regarding our serious concerns over Brother Lee and his son, Philip, who had managed the LSM office. He told us that Brother Lee himself was now managing the LSM office. The matter of the sixteen points spoken on August 28th was brought up, and we explained that they were addressed to the local need and were intended for that. He remarked that he did not think they had any need of covering those same needs in Irving, at least not now. Then he proceeded to share with us some news of the full-time training that was being conducted in Irving, Texas. At that time, they had forty-two trainees in two terms of training.

CALLS RECEIVED REGARDING
THE SIXTEEN POINTS

September - November 1988

Soon after the August 28th meeting, saints began to visit us and call on the phone, some bothered by implications they felt were made, and some very happy and thankful for what was spoken. Copies of the edited transcript were soon received in other places. Some went to the Cleveland, Ohio area, and Titus Chu, the leading coworker in that area, called, quite alarmed over this. He said that if they had been sent only to the leading ones that would have been different, but they were being sent to ordinary saints who were being disturbed by them. He asked that we halt the dissemination of this material, though we had sent none.

I called a brother who I thought may have sent copies to the Ohio area, since he used to live there and knew a number of saints. He had done it, and I asked him if he would cease, because it was causing trouble. The brother replied that because I asked him to stop sending them, he would send them out now by the thousands, and he strongly rebuked me for my weakness in not standing for the truth before brothers like Titus.

ELDERS MEETING IN ATLANTA

September 1988

In September Brother Lee had a conference in Atlanta with two elders' meetings, one on Friday, September 16th, and the other on the Lord's Day, September 18th. The second meeting was exceptional with brothers from all over the country attending. I would like to briefly describe it, noting a few significant things that were said, (I myself was not present but I received reports from a number of brothers concerning it.)

Brother Lee strongly vindicated the way he had taken against all criticisms. He drew a line; any who would not take this way, he said, are "dropouts", and the Lord will have no mercy. Addressing the brothers, he said that none of them understood what he was doing. None knew what he was doing in Taipei; hence there was no one that he could fellowship with. When I went to Taipei, he said, I did not fellowship with one person concerning what I was going to do. He continued: None of you is perfected. Who can say that he is perfected? So you are not qualified to criticize what I am doing. I didn't include you in my fellowship – how can I? So let there be no more talk about anything I do. You criticize my young trainers in Taipei, telling me their mistakes, but I was doing everything; what they did was to carry out my burden.

I want to comment here on what I consider to be a very serious lack of fellowship. Every one of us, from the smallest member to the largest, needs the fellowship of the Body for a safeguard and balance. For example, I feel that in Taiwan had Brother Lee had more fellowship, especially with the older brothers, many problems could have been eliminated. But the older elders and co-workers who had labored diligently to build up the churches were put aside and much younger brothers, novices, were brought into the inner circle. I am reminded of Rehoboam, the son of Solomon, who instead of receiving the counsel of the older men who had stood before Solomon his father, he forsook them and followed the counsel of the young men who had grown up with him (2 Chron. 10:6-11). His choice was disastrous and resulted in a great division in Israel. I fear that history has been repeated.

The elders' meeting in Atlanta went on from 4:00 P.M. till 8:00 P.M. with Brother Lee speaking for close to three and a half hours. At the end he told what a great success the work had been in Taipei in the recent years. They had gained their objectives, and now they were going to evangelize the entire island. He then asked Benson to outline the plans for doing this.

Don Rutledge, an elder in Dallas before moving to North Carolina, told me, "That meeting was the most devastating and discouraging experience of all my time in the church." What particularly bothered him was Brother Lee's attitude toward the brothers. The atmosphere, he said, was heavy, oppressive, and abusive. (Reports came to my ears from a number of brothers who attended that meeting; all indicated something similar.) Brother Lee had wanted to have a time of fellowship with Don immediately following the session, but Don was so troubled and depressed that he told Brother Lee he had to go home. As he walked out the door, Titus Chu came up and said to Don, "I'm afraid this will make our situation worse. I hope not."

A few months later at the elders' meetings in Irving, Texas, Don Rutledge asked Titus, "Why did we need such a meeting as that?" Titus told him that it was because of one brother who was present in that meeting – a former elder in the church in San Jose. Brother Lee had been informed concerning him that he was going from house to house influencing people against his ministry (which was not true).

FURTHER CONFERENCES

May – June 1988

During the months of May and June 1988 I was asked to minister in a number of places, in almost all of which I was burdened to share from the Lord's word to the seven churches in Revelation 2 and 3. We emphasized the need to come back to the beginning, saying that the way for us to go on is to come back – back to the living person of Christ as the tree of life. We also spoke in some places concerning the need for local administration in the churches to preserve the Lord's headship as we did in Miami. Some saints who were in these conferences were disturbed because we were not speaking exactly the same things as Brother Lee concerning the "new way", although we certainly were not teaching anything different from God's economy, Christ and the church.

The brothers in Orange County, California, were desirous of having a conference and arranged for one meeting to be held in Long Beach (Friday night), another in Huntington Beach (Saturday night), and the last in Irvine (Lord's Day evening). This transpired over the weekend of June 3-5, 1988. The Lord's blessing was on these meetings as we spoke here locally the same as we had spoke in other churches elsewhere: coming back to the beginning, Christ as our unique Head and center, and local administration and universal mutual fellowship. In Irvine we also stressed the need of all the saints to feed richly on the Word of God for the building up of the church.

Attending the conference meeting in Irvine were Joseph Fung of Hong Kong and Paul Ma of Santa Cruz, California. It was the first time I had seen these brothers in years, and I did not know just where they stood in regard to the concerns we had. They, on the other hand, did not know where I stood. They asked to have a time of fellowship with me the next day, Monday, June 6th, at which time I testified to them what we realized and passed through in recent months. They fully echoed our concerns. I was impressed to learn that Joseph Fung, as well as many others in the Far East had the same burden and realization as we had. This was an encouragement and strengthening.

The brothers in Anaheim wanted me to share the Word in a little conference there. This I did in two meetings, Saturday evening and the Lord's Day morning, June 18th and 19th. On Saturday evening we ministered from Ezra on leaving Babylon (which had been manifested in the confusion, division, and depression among us in Anaheim) and returning to Jerusalem to build the house of the Lord. There was a strong sense of the Lord's speaking and presence, and the sharings of the saints were excellent and very inspiring.

ADDITIONAL FELLOWSHIP WITH BROTHER LEE

June 20, 22, 1988

On Monday morning June 20th, Brother Lee called us – Godfred, Al, and me – to come to his home for further fellowship that night. Due to the restrictions of my health, I told Brother Lee that I would have to leave by 10:00 P.M., knowing how easy it is for such meetings to be prolonged late into the night. He replied that there would be no problem, that the meeting would probably be concluded by 8:30 P.M. During this time, he especially mentioned he had recently received complaining about my speaking in various conferences. He rose out of his seat and went into his office, bringing back with him a file folder which he reported was full of letters concerning my speaking. We could only see it across the room at a distance, and it appeared to contain a large amount of 8 ½ x 11 paper, which I assumed to be transcripts of some of my messages sent to him by saints desiring to express their loyalty and faithfulness to his ministry. I was not surprised. Such a reaction was inevitable considering the concept governing the saints. We went on to discuss the current problems.

The hours passed as I was certain they would, and it was soon 10:00 P.M. I was already worn out, so I asked the brothers if they would please excuse me according to my word. As I rose to leave, Brother Lee turned to me and asked me to forgive him for anything he had done over the years that may have offended me, thinking that my speaking in the conferences was occasioned by some offense I suffered from him. His voice broke as he spoke. I assured him that what I said was due to nothing, whatever of that nature, and that I had no personal problem with him at all, but rather that I spoke out of genuine concern for the truth. He abruptly dropped the matter, and turning to the other brothers he changed the subject. I then departed, leaving Brother Lee, Godfred, and Al engaged in further discussion.

Godfred and Al continued their fellowship with Brother Lee until 11:00 P.M., the content of which was reported to me the next morning by Godfred. I was told that at one point in answer to Brother Lee's inquiry, asking what we should do to deal with the issues, Godfred proposed that a number of brothers come together with Brother Lee for several days to confront the issues in fellowship and arrive at a satisfactory resolution. At first Brother Lee was not receptive, feeling that because of what had transpired he would not have the ground with certain brothers to invite them to come. Then he suggested that both he and ourselves could sign a letter of invitation to make it more acceptable to come. This satisfied him, and he became very favorable to the proposition. But no definite decision was made that night, as Godfred and Al said that they would have to speak with me about the matter.

Upon hearing Godfred's proposal the next morning, I had a deep sense of apprehension and was reluctant to agree. Yet since the brothers felt to proceed in this direction I forced myself to go along. Brother Lee called Godfred that morning to learn what decision was made, and Godfred told him he would have to call me, which he did. We talked about the matter and came up with names of about fifteen elders and leading co-workers throughout the United States and Europe who would be invited. Brother Lee then suggested that some time after the summer training would be suitable for him and that we should decide what days would suit us and let him know. He would then try to arrange his schedule accordingly. I agreed very reluctantly, that we would do this.

During the following days I considered the whole matter at length and after much thought felt deeply that it would not be profitable for the truth's sake, and that however misunderstood we may be we should not proceed. We had already met with Brother Lee a good number of times, opening to him and expressing our concerns to him, and made very little progress. Moreover, we feared, from past experience, that if we had such a meeting Brother Lee would dominate it, overwhelm us, and eventually whitewash the issues. Frankly speaking, my trust in Brother Lee, which had once been so high was greatly reduced; he had lost much of his credibility with me. I shared my conclusion with Godfred and Al, and they agreed not to go ahead with it. We did not, however, communicate with Brother Lee immediately. Later, when he inquired concerning the matter I told him that we felt not to proceed.

A little while afterwards, when speaking on the phone with one of the elders in Long Beach, I told him of the proposal and our decision. He agreed with me that it would not be profitable. But his concurrence did not influence me; I was already convinced.

Since Brother Lee had expressed the thought that some sort of personal offense had given rise to my speaking, I felt it would be profitable to have an additional time to open again to him my burden and concern, indicating that I was only concerned with the truth and its practice and that there was no personal problem involved. I called him the day following our last visit and proposed another meeting together, this time with just the two of us. He welcomed my proposal, expressing his desire that we should meet. The next morning, Wednesday, June 22nd, we sat down together in his home. Again, I covered with Brother Lee in a rather full and complete way all my anxieties concerning the churches and the work, speaking frankly and trying to make my feelings clear. Brother Lee heard me out, but it seemed that he was merely tolerating me and what I had to say. He had little to say in response. It was not encouraging. At the end of the time I remarked that unless he would have some change it would be difficult for the churches to go on. This was now the twelfth session that I had with Brother Lee since December 12th, 1987, either individually or with others. It was about this time that Brother Lee notified us that he had discharged Philip Lee from the management of the Living Stream Office, stating that it was a very hard step for him to take.

SUMMER TRAINING AND ELDERS' MEETINGS IN ANAHEIM

July 1988

The summer training began in Anaheim on June 29th and covered the first part of Leviticus. Godfred had no heart to attend the training, I attended part time mornings, and Al Knoch attended full time. We were troubled by the way Brother Lee used some of the messages to deal with the present situation. He was obviously preoccupied by it. This was the last training of Brother Lee's that I ever was to attend.

Following the training Brother Lee called for two elders' meetings to be held on Saturday morning, July 9th. There were approximately four hundred elders and learning elders present. Brother Lee gave two messages: in the first he spoke on God's administration and addressed the matters of "autonomy" and "federation". This was a very clear reference to the things I had spoken regarding the local administration of the churches, warning against the dangers of church affiliation or federation, which lead to central control and denominationalism. Brother Lee believed strongly that my stress on local administration would lead to the independence of all the local churches. As a matter of fact, I never once in all my speaking used the word "autonomy." But in Brother Lee's own publication, The Beliefs and Practices of the Local Churches, the word "autonomy" is used positively two times. I believe Brother Lee felt that, by my speaking, his concept of all the local churches moving and acting as one body under his leadership was threatened. Therefore, he fought against the imagined devil, autonomy, in every conference of his for months to come, referring to it as a wind of teaching brought in by the sleight of men to fabricate a system of error.

The word "federation," which I did indeed use, offended him greatly. He believed I was classifying all the local churches under his leadership as a federation, whereas he insisted they were the "organic Body of Christ." He began to use the word "organic" frequently. I wish the churches were so organic. We were witnessing so much that was absolutely inorganic among the churches, things that were rather organizational and exhibiting signs of a hierarchy, for example in the FTTT. Therefore, I warned the saints against a kind of federation. Actually, I used the word "affiliation" much more, which is a milder form of federation, but nonetheless fraught with perils. The local churches had surely become an affiliation.

We had seen that in church history, whenever the Lord had raised up groups of His people for His testimony, they had persistently degraded into denominations; and the first two signs of this degradation were unfailingly: 1) the affiliating of the groups under a central leadership; 2) the establishing of a central training center, where their full-time workers could be educated and equipped to serve in their sphere of fellowship. When these two steps had eventualized, they were well on their way to becoming just another denomination, however advanced in the knowledge of truth they were. It was more than obvious that we in the local churches had taken those identical steps and were going down the same road. Should we remain silent?

In his second message of the elders' meetings, Brother Lee spoke concerning our going on. After all our sessions and hours of fellowship with Brother Lee, we had hoped that he would take steps to clear up a number of things publicly. This was surely an excellent opportunity, a perfect forum, and an appropriate time. He did give a few principles for our going on which would be helpful if practiced. He did say, "It is altogether wise and profitable that we do not expect all the churches to be the same," and, "Do not talk about who is for this or who is for that…We should not label ourselves or label others." We were thankful to hear these comments and urgings. But we were deeply disappointed that he did not go much further. What he should have cleared up he covered up, e.g., problems regarding the LSM office and the FTTT training in Taipei. We hoped he would have repented for some things that had caused many problems, not just for allowing saints from the U.S. to attend the training in Taiwan. We surely would have respected him had he done this, and the situation could have been altogether different than it turned out.

At the close of Brother Lee's second message, Dick Taylor (of Long Beach) and Frank Scavo (of Irvine) asked questions which Brother Lee attempted to answer. Dick's question was quite appropriate and fit our situation. It was as follows: "Many times you reach a point in your experience where you have genuine concerns. How can you fellowship about these concerns without being considered as negative and thereby causing another problem? This is a concern to me, and this is related to the freedom of seeking the Lord and the truth." In Brother Lee's response he said that if you have a genuine concern for anyone in regard to the Lord's recovery you should go to him alone without talking to anyone else. Any "pre-talk", he said, opens the door for the devil to come in. Now this may be true in many cases, but in our history of contacting Brother Lee over our concerns we felt we could not and should not do that. Since the issues were so momentous we needed fellowship for a clearer understanding and preparation for visiting him. In fact, Brother Lee and brothers around him have also had a lot of consultation among themselves regarding concerns for other brothers before going to them. I know because I myself participated in such discussions.

Brother Lee's attitude while speaking was gentle and persuasive; he was seeking in this way to reconcile all the brothers and to set a course that would calm any fears or anxieties and eliminate any problems. Many were very happy with his fellowship; I was not at all happy or at peace.

During these elders' meetings I sat next to an elder who had spoken with me a few times previously and was very sympathetic with our concerns, having much the same concerns himself. We agreed to meet together for some fellowship that evening over dinner. This we did, and as we ate, we conversed about Brother Lee's messages that day and their impact on the situation in general. The brother felt happy and said to me, "John , I think this is the best we can expect from Brother Lee. Be thankful." I tried to be; I tried to take his view. But in the depths of my being there was a nagging disappointment. Nothing had been dealt with. No wrongs had been righted. The root was not touched. The question loomed before us, What shall we do now? I knew I had to be true to my conscience and the truth I had seen.

ANNUAL BOARD MEETING OF LIVING STREAM MINISTRY

July 15, 1988

The following week Brother Lee notified me of the annual meeting of the Board of Directors of the Living Stream Ministry. I had been a board member and the secretary of the corporation since its inception in 1968, and I still occupied these positions. The meeting was to take place at his home, Friday morning, July 15th. Present at the meeting were Brother Lee, Sister Lee, Philip Lee, Francis Ball, and myself, the five board members. Brother Lee as the president called the meeting to order and announced that the main purpose of the meeting was to elect officers for the coming year. He then nominated the following persons for election as officers: Witness Lee, president; Francis Ball, secretary; and Benson Phillips, treasurer. Brother Lee wanted to terminate my function and replace me as secretary, and I could understand that. With my present standing I was unsuited for the post, and I myself had been considering what I should do about my involvement with the LSM and when. He asked for a vote by the raising of hands, and we voted unanimously in favor of his nominations. The resolution was then made that the above mentioned brothers fill those positions for the coming year.

The position of secretary of the LSM had been for me a total rubber-stamp function. In fact, all the board members, of whom three were family members, had merely a rubber-stamp function (with the exception of Brother Lee and the possible exception of Philip Lee). In the early years of the corporation in Los Angeles in the late sixties and early seventies, the board members did participate in some amount of fellowship concerning various proposals, but in the years following that there was rarely if ever any discussion concerning any issues to arrive at a decision. I was called upon as a secretary to write the minutes of the meetings and keep the minute book in order, and also to sign important papers as the need arose. It was purely perfunctory. Brother Lee announced his intentions and decisions, and we acquiesced and fulfilled the necessary functions to make them legal. Through many years we esteemed him very highly and were content to simply do his bidding, yet knowing that it was not a normal operation. It was his business, and we were helpers.

After the vote I queried whether I should still remain on the board as a board member. Brother Lee answered that if I chose to do that it was all right with him; if I chose not to remain it was also all right. I could do whatever I felt I should do. I said then that for simplicity's sake I had better resign, and I notified him of my intention to do that. He responded that in that case I should write a letter and put it in writing. I said that I would.

After the board meeting was adjourned, Sister Lee and Philip Lee left the room, and Brother Lee continued to talk at length with Francis Ball and myself about the current situation. I just listened, saying very little. He said how much he and Philip Lee and their families had suffered through all the talk about them. He then stated,

"Philip, of course, is not perfect; nobody is perfect!" It shocked me that he would make such an inappropriate statement as that after all that had been said and done.

I went home and typed up the minutes of the meeting, my last minutes as secretary of the LSM, and turned it over to Francis Ball, the current secretary, assuring him of my willingness to help in any matter related to his assuming that function should he need it. I also typed a letter of resignation from the Board of Directors of the LSM and delivered it to Brother Lee personally the following Monday morning. As I stood at his door, I told him what it was and he received it with a noticeably pained expression on his face. It was indeed a sad occasion, the end of a certain relationship that had been maintained for many years, and it was felt. And so, for me, ended another era.

PART FOUR

A VISIT WITH TWO SENIOR CO-WORKERS FROM TAIWAN

November 1988

During the past year I had heard of two senior co-workers from Taiwan who were living in the San Francisco Bay Area, Brothers Chu Shun Min and Jeng Guang Ming, and I longed to have fellowship with them. I had first met Brother Chu in Kaohsiung, Taiwan, in 1965, and had seen him a few times since then at conferences and trainings. Although I did not know him well, I had heard of his fruitful labors in Taiwan to build up the churches, especially in Kaohsiung and Taipei. Brother Jeng, I had also met many years ago and was aware of his labor for the Lord in Bangkok and other places. The turmoil in Anaheim having grown and intensified, I was especially burdened to see them, having heard of their burden and concern for the present situation.

Thus, on November 9th I flew to San Francisco and was met by Brother Jeng and Brother Daniel Wu, a former co-worker in Manila, who was living in the South San Francisco area. They transported me to Brother Jeng's home in Los Altos, where for three days I met with the brothers. They were intensely interested in the progress of events in Anaheim, and I opened freely and fully to them. Likewise, Brothers Chu and Jeng opened freely and fully to me regarding their convictions and concerns for the churches and the work of the Lord. I would like to share in some detail their fellowship with me, beginning with Brother

Chu Shun Min, who had been closely related to Brother Witness Lee since the revival in Chefoo in 1943 and the ensuing years. He knew Brother Lee and his family very well.

Brother Chu began by saying that he hoped that Brother Lee would have some change, but he had not seen a trace of this. Only a few know the source and the gravity of the problem. The reasons, he stated, for the present degraded situation of the churches were as follows:

1. Brother Lee's position among the churches was overly exalted. The matter of greatest concern is that he would be idolized and thus replace the position of the Lord and the Holy Spirit in the church.

2. Brother Lee's teachings and messages were overly read and repeated in the churches, causing us to be concerned that the position of God's Word would be replaced. The words of man flourishes, and the Word of God languishes. The opportunities for the Holy Spirit to speak are scarce. These first two points are the fundamental problems.

3. Brother Lee's leading has become a factor of discord and even of division among the brothers and sisters (e.g., door-knocking). Originally his leading was a factor of oneness.

4. Today we have overemphasized deputy authority more than the Bible teaches. The result is that people follow blindly and damage the Lord's testimony. Obedience is a spiritual virtue, but we must be very careful lest we damage the Lord's testimony through blind submission. Those who coordinated with Brother Lee in the past all learned the lesson of submission, but they were overly submissive with a tendency to exalt man. That caused trouble. The co-workers did this, and they led the saints also to do this. Thus, the co-workers bear the responsibility for damaging the testimony.

5. Today there are too many practices that are not according to the truth. It was because of the truth that Paul resisted Peter, as recorded in Galatians 2. Today we don't stand for the truth, but talk about deputy authority and raise up a pope. Thus, the Holy Spirit is much restricted in the church. We talk about the Holy Spirit, but we don't have the Spirit. We should only submit to the Spirit.

6. In many churches Brother Lee only set up as elders those who fully followed him. They are the ones who will execute his strategy. He did not consider whether those ones were immature or not; he only considered whether they would listen to him. Therefore, someone called them "baby elders." Those who were experienced in the Lord, those who possessed the qualities of an elder and were manifested as such, were set aside.

7. Brother Lee's leading was intended to help and supply the churches. However, unfortunately, he eventually used all kinds of methods to control: the ministry office, the trainings, the elders' meetings, etc. He utilizes the simplicity of the brothers and sisters as a means of control. He controls the full-timers to influence the rest of the saints. He uses some of his writings and the way of reading.

8. Deviations in Brother Lee's leading:

a) He causes the saints to overemphasize his writings (e.g. Life Studies, Truth Lessons, Life Lessons, etc.), leading to a reduction in the reading of the Lord's Word.

b) He causes the saints to overemphasize prayreading and calling on the Lord (matters which are meant to help the saints), leading to a reduction of genuine prayers to the Lord. The result is that the brothers and sisters do not know how to pray, and those who are newly saved do not learn how to pray.

c) He overemphasizes and twists the matter of meetings in 1 Corinthians 14 so that the function of those members who can speak for the Lord as mouths in the Body is gradually diminished. Thus, no gifts and functions are produced. I would like now to record some of the comments made by Brother Jeng Guang Ming. He spoke as follows:

We co-workers in the past have not had genuine fellowship among us concerning any questionable practices in the churches due to the prevailing concept that we should have no opinion, but rather just listen and submit. Brother Lee has related his experience and attitude toward Brother Nee in order to kill all opinions as well as all feelings and concerns. But our genuine fellowship is in sharing the feelings the Lord gives us, and in this we discover the leading of the Holy Spirit.

SPEAKING THE TRUTH IN LOVE

I very much treasure Acts 13, where the Holy Spirit spoke, "Separate unto me Barnabas and Saul for the work to which I have called them." I believe that the speaking of the Holy Spirit to the brothers there in Antioch must have been through the genuine fellowship of the feelings which the Holy Spirit Himself gave to them. The same thing occurred in Acts 15. As long as the Holy Spirit speaks among us there will be no problem. But we don't have today the leading of the Holy Spirit as in Acts 13 and 15, a leading in fellowship, a subjective leading manifested by each one speaking his own feeling before the Lord. The plurality gives the Holy Spirit opportunity. If we emphasize the one leadership so much how can the Holy Spirit have opportunity? The Spirit's leading in the Body is in the prayer and fellowship of all. The kind of submission being practiced today kills the move of the Holy Spirit in the churches through the genuine fellowship among the saints.

We have no intention to rebel or overthrow Brother Lee. We have suppressed our feeling for many years, though we sensed there were many points of deviation. In Taiwan Brother Chu and I had no such fellowship concerning the abnormal situation in the churches today as we now have. We feel that the genuine fellowship must be like that recorded in Revelation chapters 2 and 3, where the Lord did not refrain from pointing out the negative aspects as well as the positive, the real situation.

One basic item of the change in nature in the Lord's recovery is that it appears the Lord's work has become Brother Lee's work; the churches have become Brother Lee's churches; and the Lord's workers have become Brother Lee's workers. All things have become personalized, and everything appears to require Brother Lee's approval to be legitimate. He can acknowledge and he can also deny the validity of the Lord's workers, elders, and even churches. This concept has been injected to all the brothers and sisters, particularly those who have a heart for the Lord. This is how denominations are formed. But the Lord had preserved some for Himself. This situation did not develop suddenly, and we cannot expect it to clear up suddenly.

Brother Chu Shun Min then told me how that on April 1, 1988, he had a conversation with Brother Lee in the Bay Area. He presented a number of serious concerns to Brother Lee and asked him to bring all these things to the Lord. Brother Chu told me that Brother Lee listened quietly and passively to all his points (with one exception), making no comment, neither admitting nor denying. The exception was a point he made concerning Brother Lee's son, Philip Lee. In conclusion, Brother Chu told Brother Lee, "All the sweet feeling we had in the past is lost. All the rest in our spirit is over."

I will mention just a few more comments made by Brother Chu. He said that he feels very sorry for the present state of things -- he gave his whole life to this. He has received letters from elderly ones in Taipei that are full of blood and tears. There are very few elderly people there who are not discouraged or withdrawn. The warfare now is fiercer than in Watchman Nee's day when the issue was that of leaving the denominations. We are at a critical juncture. We cannot be silent regarding the change of nature in the Lord's recovery. We should have no part in it. This is a day for further recovery. We need a new beginning to recover us back from the change of nature to the Lord's original intention. We must discard all the changes of nature. The main direction is to come out of the system; it cannot change.

I greatly respected these brothers for their years of faithful labor, their knowledge of the Lord and His ways, their maturity in Christ, and their penetrating discernment. Their fellowship was a strong confirmation and encouragement to be steadfast for the truth's sake. It seemed outwardly that Brothers Chu and Jeng were in a state of retirement from the work, but inwardly they were active and aggressive, praying and watching and fighting in the spiritual warfare. I have been greatly inspired by them. They count very much for the Lord's interests.

CONFERENCE AND ELDERS' MEETING IN PASADENA

November 1988

On the Thanksgiving Day weekend of November 1988 Brother Lee, just returned from Taiwan, held a conference of five meetings in the auditorium of the Pasadena City College in California. The conference was followed by an elders' meeting November 27th in the meeting place of the church in San Gabriel. In that meeting Brother Lee proclaimed that though he had a hall in Anaheim, he was not happy to use it (no doubt because of certain people who were in Anaheim). The brothers in the Los Angeles area invited him to have a conference and arranged the place in Pasadena. He said that when he heard that it would be in Pasadena, he was happy. These people, he said, "exalt" me: I am happy to be exalted.

Before the conference began a report came to us that a flyer had been printed and would be placed on the windshields of all the cars of those attending the conference in Pasadena. On the flyer, we were told, some sinful disorders were mentioned. We fully disapproved of such action. Not knowing who authorized or printed them or who intended to distribute them, but knowing a couple of brothers who we thought might be aware of it, we called them and urged them to do whatever they could to stop the distribution. It seems that our word was heeded, at least to some extent, for no flyers were distributed at the conference. We discovered later, however, that they were put on some cars in the Anaheim meeting hall parking lot. Such acts we believe to be of the flesh and not the way to protest wrongdoing. Some time later, after the conference, we obtained a copy of the flyer. It was entitled Significant Dates in the History of the Church in Anaheim.

In the first meeting of the conference, November 25th, Brother Lee was in a fighting spirit, fighting against "autonomy" and "federation." He referred to some books authored by George Henry Lang, a servant of the Lord in England during the latter part of the 19th century and the first half of the 20th. In one of his books, entitled The Churches of God, Lang emphasized the need for local administration in the churches. This was the book that troubled Brother Lee. (I had read this book, and being deeply impressed with its strong scriptural basis and timely application to our present need, I had recommended it to others.) Brother Lee called Lang's book heretical and told the saints if they had them to burn them. I consider this kind of talk reckless and lawless. Brother Lee in years past had commended Lang for his insight and writing on the truth of the kingdom. His books have been recently reprinted and are available today.

In the conference meetings he strongly vindicated himself and his work. He gave a message in which he recounted a number of revelations brought forth by him which he said no one else besides the Bible authors had ever seen. Regarding the enjoying of Christ he said, "I invented this term, enjoying Christ." He continued, "I invented this term, experiencing Christ, exhibiting Christ." I believe a number of saints could testify that they heard of enjoying Christ or enjoying the Lord long before Brother Lee ever came to the United States. I for one did. My stepmother, seeking to help me, spoke to me about this in 1949. No doubt she heard this from other Christian teachers. The term, experiencing Christ, has also been spoken by other Christian teachers for years. Brother Lee did not invent that term. He mentioned many other items, claiming that they had all been revealed to him in the past twenty or so years; no one else had ever seen or spoken of them.

He referred to the title he has used for the Holy Spirit – "the all-inclusive Spirit of Christ as the consummation of the processed Triune God" – and asked who made such a title. Webster? he asked. Then he answered his own question, "That Lee! Lee has to be famous! Lee! Lee! Lee must have the credit! And if you listen to me, you do not listen to

Lee, you listen to the very God in His oracle spoken by me." A little later in his message he said, "Going with God's oracle, surely there is the deputy authority of God in this oracle. Whoever speaks for God, he surely has certain divine authority. I'm claiming this for Lee!"

Now I would ask, are these the words of a sober man, the words of a spiritual man, a man of God? To me it is shocking to hear him speak this way, for he has indeed been used of God in the past to speak His Word. But to vindicate oneself so blatantly and boastfully indicates to me a fall. May the Lord have mercy on us all.

Following his message, he asked for testimonies to be given by brothers from five countries: Brazil, the Philippines, Korea, Taiwan, and the United States. All these told of the success of the new way in their place, especially giving statistics regarding the number of churches and new ones baptized. The Lord along knows the real situation. If there is any real blessing from Him, we rejoice and give thanks.

In the elders' meeting following the conference Brother Lee read from a list of items, mentioning what he said were the top ten revelations received by him, seen previously by no one else. Some of them were as follows:

1. "The last Adam became a life-giving Spirit" (1 Cor. 15:45)

2. "He who is joined to the Lord is one spirit" (1 Cor. 6:17).

3. Prayreading.

4. Calling on the name of the Lord.

5. The seven Spirits.

6. The dispensing of the processed Triune God into the tripartite man.

7. The New Jerusalem as a corporate man.

8. The lampstand as the embodiment of the Triune God.

Now we thank God for these revelations from His holy Word, but to claim that he was the first one to see these is going altogether too far. Moreover, concerning at least a number of these items, Brother

Lee was in fact not the first to see them. Regarding the last Adam becoming a life-giving Spirit and our being one spirit with the Lord, there were a number of other Christian teachers who saw and wrote of these things. We have evidence of this. Concerning prayreading, many have seen this and practiced this, as recorded in the book authored by Ray Graver and published by the LSM entitled, Lord...Thou Saidst. Calling on the name of the Lord was not a recent discovery by Brother Lee or by us. The New Jerusalem as a corporate person was also seen by others—T. Austin-Sparks for one. If we have time or if there is a need, we may document all these instances.

The revelations mentioned are indeed great and precious. Fairly speaking, some of these matters may have been fresh revelations to Brother Lee. The Lord alone knows. And some of them, he may have enunciated more clearly than his predecessors. But for anyone to claim that no one had ever seen these things before, but him, is totally insupportable, since we are not omniscient. Moreover, such self-vindication is very unbecoming and repugnant.

Brother Lee went on to say, "You cannot deny the fact that the Lord's oracle has been with me. I claim this at the face of Jesus Christ. The deputy authority of God is in His oracle; so whoever speaks for God has His deputy authority. But I never used it."

In the elders' meeting, Brother Lee referred to some anonymous papers being circulated and blamed the elders in Anaheim for not stopping the distribution. He then referred to the flyer which had been printed and was to be put on the windshields of the cars at the conference. I then rose from my seat and said that we wanted Brother Lee and all the brothers to know that we fully disapproved of that action and had done whatever we could to stop it. Brother Lee took the opportunity then, while I was on my feet, to question me publicly about a few things. He asked me about an anonymous writing entitled Reconsidering Our Vision. (which had troubled him greatly) and if we had done anything to stop its circulation. I said that we had not.

Regarding some brothers, probably including me (or, especially me), Brother Lee said, "Whether you are for me or not, I know; I know everything. I know what restaurant you were eating in, what day, and with whom. I have a lot of colleagues who write me long records of ten to twenty pages about you." He said further, "Which church is under my hand? You have a church; I have none. I know which church welcomes me, and which has a cold heart toward me."

Near the end of his word he proclaimed, "I don't care for the loss of any church. Even if the entire U. S. A. is closed to me, I don't care. I only care for ten to twenty faithful ones meeting together to practice the truth. "

When he sat down and asked for fellowship, a brother from Anaheim, Paul Kerr, rose toward the end of the time and asked two questions. The first consisted of two queries: Why have other brothers besides you not been raised up? And, Why do you have no contemporaries to challenge you and fellowship with you? Brother Lee's answer was simply, "I don't know." And then he said that since 1945 he has been watching to see if anyone else could speak God's word as God's oracle. He could find none. Paul Kerr's next question concerned John So and John Ingalls. He asked, "How is it that in the past you referred to these two brothers as pillars and today's Timothy, and today you have nothing good to say about them?" Brother Lee's reply was that brothers can change. Demas loved the Lord, but then he changed and loved the world. I can change, he said; we all can change. So, we all need the Lord's mercy.

Brother Lee was beside himself in this meeting. I had never personally observed him in such a state as I witnessed him there. He was obviously exceedingly agitated. That was the last elders' meeting with Brother Lee that I ever attended.

HELP AND ENCOURAGEMENT RECEIVED FROM JOSEPH FUNG

December 1988 to February 1989

In the beginning of December Joseph Fung from the church in Hong Kong came to Anaheim and rendered much help and encouragement to Al Knoch and me and to a good number of other brothers and sisters in Southern California. He shared with us his testimony of the trials he passed through in Hong Kong and how he had almost resigned as an elder; how there was much maneuvering to remove him; and how by his staying on as an elder the situation in the church has been preserved and now is very healthy and living, all the church being in one accord. We prayed much together for the situation in Anaheim and were strengthened in the Lord. Both Al and I felt that the Lord had sent him to us at this time. We found him to be a brother who was faithful to his convictions and to the truth of the Word, come what may. We also observed how he loved the brothers and sisters and poured out his life for the Lord's testimony.

On Saturday evening, December 3rd, Joseph met with thirty of the saints who had been very aggressive and vocal in the meetings to speak out against the evils which they felt needed to be righted. Joseph was much anointed and was enabled to render some very positive help to them. All the saints ere deeply touched.

TELEPHONE CONVERSATION
WITH BROTHER LEE

Dec. 13, 1988

On December 6 Brother Lee called, saying that he would like to meet with Al Knoch and me before he went to Irving, Texas for the training on December 14. He hoped to meet with us on Saturday, December 10th. I told him that we felt we needed to pray more and wait for some time before having further fellowship with him, but he was rather insistent. On December 12 he called again, and then again on December 13, at which times I told him that we still felt it better that we pray more and wait for a time. He said that there were a number of points which he desired to share with us. Finally, I asked if he could just share them with me over the phone, and he agreed. I relate them as follows in Brother Lee's words in a somewhat abridged form:

1. Take my word, I have no intention of doing anything bad to you. I have prayed, Preserve my brother's usefulness in Your hand. I don't like to see any part damaged.

2. Regarding the translation work on the revision of the Recovery Version, I never had any feeling that I would give you up. I prayed about the work being moved to Irving, and I believe that was the wisdom of the Lord. I like to get this work done in a peaceful and happy way. I never said anything bad about your part. I told the brothers just recently that the whole recovery is indebted to John for his work on the hymnbook and his polishing of other books for publishing. Now I have received a letter from you saying that you would withdraw from

the work. I don't know what to say. Now that you would stop, who can continue? It is much better to get one thing done by the same person. I still would ask you to do this work, and I beg you to reconsider. This work is not only for the saints in the Lord's recovery, but for the Lord's people as a whole. Please do not think that you will be doing anything for me, but for the Lord's interests on the whole earth. I must have a definite word from you.

I told him that I had already given much consideration to this matter before writing the letter of resignation from the work.

3. Regarding the flyer that has been circulated, you said that you have stopped it, but on the Lord's Day it was distributed in the Anaheim meeting hall after the meeting. A sister was holding a bundle of them and giving them out to some of the saints. The saints in Fullerton also got copies. My name is printed on that flyer in a very negative sense. Since I am a brother in Anaheim and such a thing is still going on, I ask you as a brother in the church where I meet to take care of this. You have already had an excommunication [to deal with the problem]; so that's it! Why is such a flyer put out?

4. On August 28th you put out sixteen points, eight by you and eight by Godfred. I wanted to fellowship with you about these points, but I did not have time. After the coming training in Irving, I hope to sit down with you to study some of these points. They were sent out to all the churches. One brother told me that they were sixteen bullets aimed at me to put me aside from the church in Anaheim or from the Lord's recovery.

5. At the end of the training in Irving there will be some elders' meetings. So many elders will attend. I am burdened in those meetings to speak something very positive and give the Lord a way to lead us on positively. We will not go back to touch the things that have happened in the past. (Note: See under the following sub-title the contents of these elders' meetings.) The present situation is damaged and divided. The Lord's recovery was brought to this country through me, and you were the first one to take this way. Our hearts have been for the Lord's recovery, and I believe you still have such a heart. I ask you to please go to Irving for the elders' meetings. I believe they will be a great help,

resulting in a very positive and profitable issue. We must endeavor to give the Lord a way. Brother Lee told me that he had called other brothers in Orange County encouraging them to go. I know that he also called Bill Mallon. I myself was not led of the Lord to go.

6. Very honestly, not only as a brother, but as a friend, I want to speak to you about Joseph Fung. It is very hard for me to say anything bad about anyone. But he was spreading the news that Hong Kong and Rosemead were genuine local churches. The genuine local churches were more than one hundred, Joseph said. All the others were ministry churches. He indicated that the churches in Southeast Asian countries, excluding the Philippines, all joined together with the churches in Europe to be against me. (Note: This includes Brother Lee's interpretation of what Joseph said. Joseph never said that any church, including Hong Kong, was against Brother Lee.)

Brother Lee then told me what someone had expressed to him in regard to Joseph Fung, which was not positive. To this day, however, I still thank the Lord for Joseph and honor him in the Lord. I thanked Brother Lee for his concern, and we said goodbye. That was the last time I spoke with Brother Lee.

ELDERS' MEETINGS IN IRVING, TEXAS

Dec. 31, 1988 – Jan 2, 1989

In the elders' meetings in Irving, following the winter training, there were 340 elders present, a large number, and Brother Lee spoke to them on the following four points:

1. Gospel preaching: door-knocking is the best way.

2. Home visitation for meetings with the new ones.

3. Mutuality in the meetings.

4. Church meetings for building up.

Brother Lee had spoken many, many times on these same things before; so there was no new light or direction. When I heard the contents of the meetings, I felt confirmed in my not going.

At the close of the elders' meetings, Francis Ball, a long time elder and co-worker with us, rose and proposed a nationwide day of fasting and prayer on January 11th, to pray especially for the critical condition of the recovery and the churches. He then turned to Brother Lee and asked if he would approve of it. Brother Lee responded by saying that the condition of the recovery was not that bad, and what we were experiencing was only a passing storm. Then he said that only Germany and Anaheim have problems due to the danger of changing the truth.

I considered Brother Lee's singling out of these two places and his charging them with being in danger of changing the truth to be serious. I would like to know what truth we have ever changed or are in danger of changing. Rather we have sought to be faithful to the truth, much of which we have seen through the help of Brother Lee's ministry. Our problem in the past has been related not mainly to the truth itself, but to its practice, which we are seeking diligently to remedy. However, one crucial matter affecting the truth I will mention here. In Ephesians 4 there are seven factors of our oneness and only seven. But today other factors, at least in practice, have been added, such as, one ministry, one leadership, one deputy authority, and one divine oracle. These have been made factors of our oneness, so that if any individuals or churches do not adhere to the "one ministry", or the "one leadership", etc., they are cut off or labeled negatively. Now, is this not true? We have many examples to substantiate it.

Brother Lee has told the brothers who were serving with him a number of times, including myself, that if he ever left the way of God's recovery, we should not follow him; rather we should go forward according to the truth to follow the Lord. We believe that in some degree this very thing has occurred, and we are taking Brother Lee's own word to go on in the truth. May the Lord grant us mercy and grace to be faithful.

NEWSPAPER ARTICLES APPEAR

January 1989

On Saturday, January 7th, 1989, in the religious section of the Los Angeles Times, the first article regarding the problems among us appeared. It was rather long, covering two columns, and was entitled Crisis Threatens Future of Little-Known Church. It referred to the publication of an anonymous twenty-page pamphlet critical of Brother Lee and quoted from it. It stated that Philip Lee is a "powerful figure in the church second only to his father." Worst of all it mentioned some charges of sinful acts taking place. This is what we had feared most of all for over a year and had warned Brother Lee that this might occur if nothing was done promptly to clear up the disorder. Mentioning my name, the article attributed me as saying, "the problems were best handled internally out of the public eye," and then stated that I had refused further comment.

Referring to information they had received, the writer said, "Some former members furnished The Times with transcriptions of taped emotional meetings in Anaheim and a copy of the pamphlet that has been circulated widely among church members in Taiwan and the United States." I strongly feel that such "former members" did not serve the Lord's interests well by giving out such information. It is indeed shameful that there should be any ground for such an article to appear in print in a major newspaper – shameful to Brother Lee, to his ministry, to the churches, and to all the saints. Worst of all it is a smear on the Lord's testimony.

We understand that another article regarding our problems was also printed in the Chinese World Journal, a Chinese periodical published in Monterrey Park, California, with global circulation. We did not see it, nor could we read it except by translation. It was no surprise to us to learn that Brother Lee was deeply disturbed over these two newspaper articles. There may have been more in other cities in the country that have not come to our attention.

In the fall 1988 issue of The Christian Research Institute Journal there was also an article about us entitled Turmoil in the "Local Church". It carried as well a photo of Brother Lee and his wife. This writing quotes at length from the twenty-page pamphlet mentioned above. It also speaks of various disorders that are disgraceful. I have no heart to say anymore.

A GATHERING STORM

October 1988

Beginning on the Lord's Day, September 4th, and continuing in every Lord's Day morning meeting for over a month, some of the saints in Anaheim interrupted the meeting with derogatory remarks concerning Brother Lee, even mentioning his name. Most all the saints, including ourselves, felt grieved over this, considering it to be out of place and not helping the situation. That the saints were outraged was evident; that their grievances were justifiable, we believed in major part they were; but the way they took was objectionable. This sort of activity continually worsened and became intolerable, and the number of saints attending the meetings dropped off considerably. We realized that we could not go on like that. Some felt that we needed to address the matter once for all to clear up everything, and then go on, and one troubled brother, a former full-timer, expressed that to us.

After the prayer meeting on Tuesday, September 20th, a sister in the church who worked closely with Brother Lee stood and strongly proclaimed, "We have to do some business!" (She meant that we have to deal with some matters.) She went on to say that in the last few Lord's Day meetings she had been killed (by the derogatory statements concerning Brother Lee) and she didn't want to be killed anymore. Henceforth, she said, she would stay home during the Lord's Day morning meeting, and she encouraged others to stay home as well. Others followed this sister's proclamation to confirm it and say that they also did not want to be killed. Some said that they just wanted to enjoy the Lord. Then a bold and rather outspoken sister rose and said that all that kind of talk was too petty. We need to be the Lord's testimony, she said, and then she began to mention some alleged sin in our midst. This greatly provoked some of the saints, who tried unprevailingly to stop her. Others went on to speak from conflicting viewpoints. I was the only elder present (Godfred was in Europe on a business trip, and Al was not feeling well). I did not interrupt but allowed the saints to speak freely for some time. After about 45 minutes the meeting was brought to a close. It was a stormy session.

A couple of days later Godfred returned from Europe, and I shared with him about the recent events and worsening situation we were facing. The tension was mounting each day, and the pressure from all sides was increasing. It seemed that we could not have peace until the underlying problems were dealt with. Because Godfred had returned, I felt I could leave for a few days and needed rest, and I did.

The next day, the Lord's Day, September 25th, a few saints on both sides of the issues tried to speak and bring up inciting negative matters. Godfred asked them all to sit down. "We are not here for that", he said, "We are here to get into the Word." He succeeded and peace was maintained. Godfred was much better at this sort of thing then Al or I, and we greatly appreciated his gift. But the conflict continued to mount both inwardly and outwardly and was obviously headed for some kind of climax.

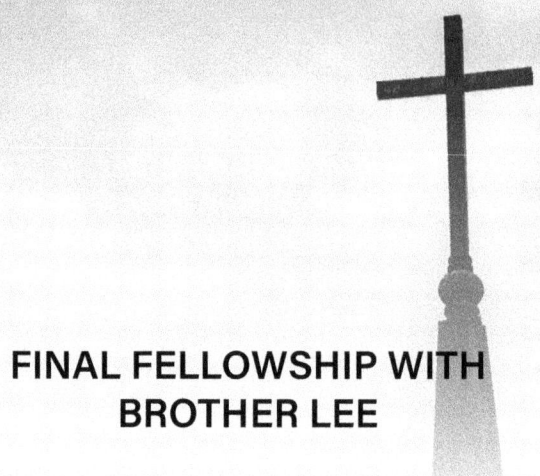

FINAL FELLOWSHIP WITH BROTHER LEE

September 28, 1988

In the midst of all this, Brother Lee called and said he desired to meet with all the elders on Wednesday evening, September28th. His main purpose was to advise us regarding the church. There were the five of us: three on the English side – Godfred, Al, and me – two on the Chinese side – Minoru Chen, and Philip Lin. He said that in the morning when he was with the Lord he thought of the story of Solomon and the baby boy, whom Solomon proposed should be divided and given to the two women who each claimed as her child. By this the true mother was discovered and the child was given to her. He said that the church in Anaheim was his baby, and that he does not like to see it suffer. He apparently had heard that some saints might come to the next Lord's Day morning meeting and explode a bomb, figuratively speaking, and he was alarmed, telling us these ones needed to be stopped. We also had heard a similar report.

Then Brother Lee spoke with us about the matter of excommunication and the need to love and care for the sinning brother, appealing to the scripture in Galatians 6:1. He was sending a message to us, for he feared that excommunication was about to be exercised upon a certain brother in the church in Anaheim.

Finally, Brother Lee showed us a letter he had just received from Germany signed by the elders of a number of churches. This letter stated that reports had been received, confirmed by several witnesses, of gross misconduct over a long period of time related to the LSM office, and that Brother Lee was aware of it and not only tolerated it, but covered it up. Because of this the churches in Europe were disassociating themselves from such misconduct in Brother Lee's work. A similar letter had been received from England. Brother Lee was greatly upset by this and he urged us – Godfred, Al, and me – to write a letter to the elders in Europe in reply, stating on his behalf that he was not aware of the misconduct and did not learn of it till December 12, 1987, when we went to him and opened up the matter. We indicated that we could not write such a letter. Since we only had it on his word that he was not aware of the matter, then he should write the letter. He said that we must rescue the churches in Europe.

He also showed us a copy of the transcript that he had just received of the sixteen points we had spoken on August 28th, just one month previously. (Actually he had requested of me a tape recording of the sixteen points the day after that meeting was, and I loaned it to him; so it was not new to him.) He mentioned that he wanted to talk with us regarding these points after he returned from his trip to Taiwan, where he was soon to go.

Brother Lee's attitude that evening was very hard, especially toward me. He was very irritated, and it was extremely difficult to reason with him. After that meeting we again felt that it was absolutely useless to have any more times of fellowship. And so it was. That was the last time we sat down with Brother Lee for face to face communication. It was the sixteenth time that I had met with him either individually or with other brothers, since December 12, 1987, nine months prior to that time, to discuss the present situation and open our hearts regarding our concerns. We had spent many hours and long sessions together concerning these matters.

The next morning Brother Lee spoke with me on the phone, saying that he reconsidered what he proposed concerning the elders writing a letter to the churches in Europe, and he felt now that we should not do it since such an act on our part would not be in nature organic.

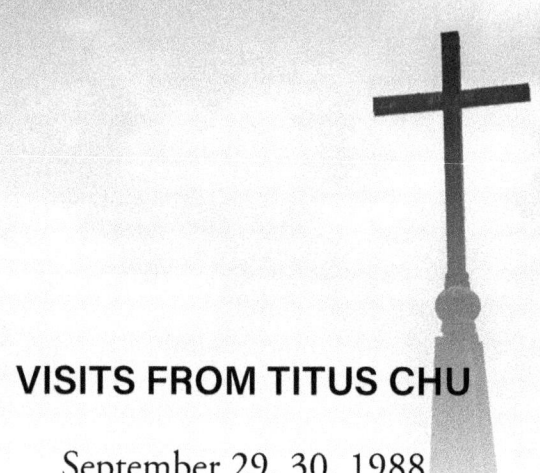

VISITS FROM TITUS CHU

September 29, 30, 1988

In December 1987, before we went to see Brother Lee on December 12th, Titus Chu was in Anaheim, and we had lunch together. At that time since I respected Titus as a senior co-worker and had considerable fellowship with him in the past, I opened to him in a general way my heavy concern for the work and the churches. He agreed with my realizations and convictions and indicated that he had the same concerns.

On Monday, September 26, 1988, Titus came to Anaheim to see Brother Lee and also wanted to see me. I did not get back to Anaheim from a few days rest until Wednesday, September 28th. He came to the Anaheim prayer meeting on Tuesday evening and spoke with Godfred afterwards, complaining about the mailing of the transcripts of the sixteen points to Ohio and seeking information concerning a certain problem of misconduct. On Thursday morning, September 29th, the day after we had our final fellowship with Brother Lee, he came to see me and fellowship for over two hours. He was quite tender and soft and said that he fully understood what I was passing through; he had passed through a similar experience himself. He wanted to assure me that he was standing with me, and he emphasized this point. He was concerned, he said, for the going on of the churches should Brother Lee pass away. He also said that he felt that Brother Lee still had some ministry for the churches, and we must find a way to receive whatever he has. He left, asking if he could return to have further fellowship the following morning. I agreed.

The next morning, Titus came with a totally different attitude and demeanor. It seemed that he took an adversarial position, and said rather decisively that now we have to cover some practical matters. He was very strong, telling me that I had damaged the Lord's recovery by the conferences I had, and that I must not speak anything contrary to Brother Lee. He is the one carrying out the work, he said; we are his co-workers with him, and we should submit to him. He warned me that if I continued to speak as I did, I would damage myself most of all, and he would have to take some action concerning me among the churches in the Midwest. Moreover, I would lose my field for ministry because the churches would not invite me. I was surprised to hear this, for that was of no concern to me and did not influence me at all. I feel that no faithful servant of the Lord should have such a consideration, but seek to simply and faithfully follow the Lord in all things, come what may. I was not ambitious to be welcomed everywhere, and was prepared to be rejected.

Before Titus left, he urged me with much feeling to go to Brother Lee, to open myself to him, and to ask how he feels about me. I had no response at all to this, since I already had many sessions with Brother Lee, and I believed I knew what he felt about me. But because he kept repeating it, I said I would consider it. Titus returned to Cleveland and a couple of weeks later called me on the phone. I told him that I felt not to see Brother Lee as he had proposed, and he replied that that was all right and made no further mention of it. I was surprised at this, expecting that he would again urge me to see him. He wanted to assure me once more that he was standing with me – that seemed to be the main point of his call. It was a very brief conversation, lasting not more than two or three minutes.

I was surprised when nearly four months later, I received a letter from Titus, coauthored by James Reetzke (an elder in Chicago long known to me), dated February 12, 1989, in which Titus reproved me among other things for not taking his fellowship to see Brother Lee. The letter was full of rebuking and censuring concerning the conduct of the elders in Anaheim and contained this statement: "Is it not a fact that you brothers and the church in Anaheim owe him {Brother Lee} your existence?" I am grateful to Brother Lee for his love and service to the saints (including myself) in past years, and I thank the Lord for what we have received through his ministry, but we surely do not owe our existence to him – that is absurd. The source of whatever we are and have, physically or spiritually, is God and no one else.

I am still puzzled by what Titus means when he says, "I am standing with you." I can only ask, considering his words and actions, "Is this the way you stand with a person?" I refrain from saying more at this point.

THE STORM BREAKS

October 9, 16, 1988

What Brother Lee feared regarding an explosive outbreak in the Lord's Day morning meeting in Anaheim October 2nd did not materialize. It was an uneventful meeting with a good fellowship in Ephesians 1:1-14. There were no disturbances as in the previous Lord's Day meetings. But it turned out to be the calm before the storm.

The next Lord's Day morning, October 9, 1988, Godfred, Al, and I met as usual in the Elders' Room before the meeting. We were expecting to fellowship that morning regarding the last part of Ephesians chapter 1. I went upstairs to the meeting hall, the other brothers lingering behind in the Elders' Room to attend to some matter. As I reached the top of the stairs, I saw all the saints who had spoken out hotly against Brother Lee and the LSM office lined up in the rows near to the front. Some of them had ceased coming to the meetings, but this morning they were all there in force. Moreover, I saw saints from other churches entering the meeting hall whom I knew to be agitated and vocal concerning the current problems. There were some from Fullerton, Huntington Beach, Torrance, and elsewhere. I knew something was up. Obviously, others had been alerted, and they were planning to do something. I turned around and hastened down the stairs to notify Godfred and Al. This was it. We must decide what to do.

We sang a hymn or two and had some prayer as usual. Meanwhile Godfred and I were conferring together in whispers as we sat on the front row. We could just dismiss the meeting. But that, we knew, would cause a tumult to erupt. After a little consultation we felt it would be better to just let them speak and get it over with once for all, and then we could go on in the coming meetings with a good order.

Soon one of them was on his feet, a dispositionally quiet brother who had been with us in the church life since the beginning in this country and had never caused any problem. He began by saying that we are not negative, we have some genuine concerns, and to have the harmony among us we all need to know the facts and deal with them. Then he referred to misconduct in the LSM office. At this point Godfred rose to his feet and asked to say something. A number of saints thought he was about to exercise control and stop the brother from speaking, so they loudly shouted, "Let him speak! Let him speak!" There was pandemonium. Eventually Godfred was able to calm them down and then said, "All right, anyone who does not desire to hear what these saints have to say may leave the meeting. Anyone who wants to hear them may stay." About a quarter of the saints rose and walked out, and the first brother who had started to speak continued.

It was said then by these saints that since the elders had not dealt with problems publicly, they could not keep quiet. They felt fully exasperated by the elders for continually delaying to take public action against disorders, the judgment of which they felt was long overdue. Such feeling had intensified to the bursting point.

Further reference was then made to the misconduct in the LSM office, and a brother in the meeting who was a former law enforcement officer interrupted the speaker, shouting, "Did you see it? Did you see it? And indicated that if he did not see it, he should not talk about it. This ignited some other brothers, one of whom claimed to be an eyewitness, who proceeded to give detailed accounts of the misconduct in anguish and outrage, mentioning the names of involved parties. Such things never should have been spoken publicly. He said, "It's a shame for us to have to stand up here and talk like this, but if we don't do it there will never be any blessing on us, " indicating that because of a sinful situation among us, God's blessing was not with the church. These saints surely felt they had cause for action. For over two hours they went on exposing some things and accusing the elders for not having dealt with them. The elders were just as much a target of their accusations as anyone else. One sister said that "the elders were weak spiritually, psychologically, and physically," and that is why they hadn't dealt with the problems.

Eventually the meeting was brought to a close. Never in our history had there been a meeting like that. Although we sympathized with their concerns, we could not agree with their way of handling them. Yet, we allowed it to continue, and when Godfred spoke, he spoke for all of us. It was over at length, and we felt that we must now shut the door on that kind of behavior and not have it repeated again. The meeting was surely worthy of blame, but let those who shake their finger and raise their voice and write letters in reproof equally blame those responsible for the problems which were the root cause of such a meeting. If there was no ground for it, no problems of such enormous magnitude, these saints who loved the Lord's recovery and gave themselves for it, and some of whom were naturally meek and mild, would never have erupted in that way.

To our great dismay we learned later that some saints who had recorded the October 9th meeting had sent out copies of the tapes to the elders of the churches in this country. We had no idea that they intended to do this or were carrying it out, and when we heard we strongly disapproved of their action. Just recently (March 1990) we found that the one responsible for this distribution was someone in another place, another church, altogether apart from the saints in Anaheim. But he had used the P.O. Box of someone in Anaheim who was not meeting with us for a return address.

We then began to receive numerous letters from elders all over the country addressed to the elders in Anaheim, castigating us for allowing such a meeting to take place. Many of them sent a copy of their letter to Brother Lee. But I wonder what they would have done had they been in our shoes and passed through what we had passed through. It is easy to criticize from a distance (I think that many who wrote were glad to be at a distance from the church in Anaheim), but when you are in the middle of the problem and have to deal with it, it is another story.

The following Saturday, we met with some of the brothers with whom we usually met to pray (Minoru Chen and Philip Lin were not there;

we met with them on Friday nights), and we decided that we would by no means permit another meeting like that on the previous Lord's Day to take place again. If those same ones would insist on continuing, we would dismiss the meeting. The next Lord's Day morning, October 16th, the same group of saints who spoke on October 9th came again obviously to prolong their denunciations. Godfred stood at the beginning and spoke, begging them to desist and allow us to continue our study of Ephesians. They interrupted him frequently, and he patiently answered their questions. Then we proceeded to read some verses in Ephesians and in a tense atmosphere some bravely attempted to share from the Word. Eventually the saints who were intent on speaking more problematic things begin to take over the meeting with much turmoil, upon which Godfred stood and summarily dismissed the meeting. About sixty percent of those attending, including the elders, left the meeting, leaving about thirty or forty, who remained and had their own meeting.

In our absence they stood and read 1 Corinthians 5 together, and took upon themselves to excommunicate a certain brother whom they believed to be guilty of gross misconduct. The elders had not done it, so they did it. One of them then proceeded to tear up the announcements on the church bulletin board regarding the coming training and the Chinese Recovery Version, and threw in the trash some LSM books on display in the bookroom. This one called two days later and apologized for such unruly behavior, and we accepted the apology. Due to the chaotic condition, we cancelled the evening meeting at the hall and met that night in homes. That week we were contacted by those who had expressed their concerns so vocally, who said that they desired further fellowship with the elders. They had met for prayer and fellowship and felt they needed direction. We made an appointment to meet with them that Saturday evening in one of their homes. This was our third private meeting with this group, the other two, in August, having already been mentioned. They expressed their desire for the church to somehow go on from this point in time. They also protested some of the things we had said, and Godfred spoke very strongly and frankly to them, reproving them for things they had said and done. They urged the elders to take over the Lord's Day morning meetings and share some needed things with the saints.

The next Lord's Day morning, October 23rd, Godfred gave an excellent and appropriate word on the headship of Christ from Ephesians. It was well received, though he spoke strongly against exalting any worker to take the place of Christ as our Head. All blessing, he brought out, depends on His headship. Godfred ministered again the following Lord's Day from Ephesians, emphasizing the oneness of the Spirit. The number in the meeting was down to about one hundred. A number of the saints were not coming and, we believed, were attending meetings of other Christian groups. In the Lord's Table in the hall that evening there were only about fifty, probably the lowest number we had ever had.

SAINTS HOLDING A DIFFERENT VIEWPOINT

October 27, 1988

On October 27th the elders had a meeting with five concerned brothers in the church who had asked for fellowship. They had written a letter to us on October 18th in which they outlined four areas of concern:

1. They did not agree that the Lord's Day morning meeting be turned into a forum to discuss issues other than the Word of God.

2. They did not agree with the after-meeting on October 16 when a group of saints in the absence of the elders excommunicated a certain brother. They hoped that the elders would make a statement to denounce it.

3. Any problem that any elders or saints may have with Brother Lee should be settled properly and privately. They did not agree with all the public accusations toward Brother Lee and those who would receive him.

4. They did not agree that the Living Stream Ministry be made a continual issue in the church meetings.

Their special concern, they said, was how the saints could go on in this situation, and they were opening for fellowship along this line. They said, moreover, that they stood with us in this difficult time. Therefore, we met with them, addressed the issues they raised, and took the opportunity to share with them our concerns for the whole situation, agreeing with some of theirs. By this you can realize the feelings of a number of saints in the church in Anaheim who had a different view.

NEWSPAPERS CALL DESIRING INFORMATION

October 1988

On October 11, a religious editor from the Los Angeles Times called me seeking further information regarding the problems in the church and the Living Stream Ministry. It was obvious that he had received considerable input. I answered that we do have some difficulties, but that we are seeking to solve them ourselves. He asked specific questions about the LSM office and its personnel, and I refused to respond. He pledged on his own initiative not to do anything until he had contacted us first.

Just one week later, we received another call, this time from an editor of the Religious News Service, based in Philadelphia, which served some forty periodicals, if I remember the number correctly. He said he wanted information concerning the turmoil in the churches, having already received much information including some transcripts. I would make no comment.

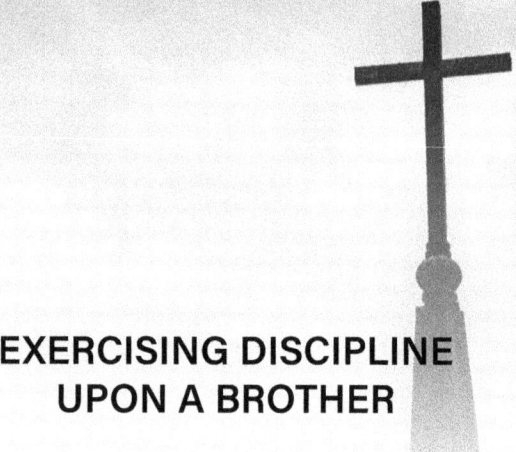

EXERCISING DISCIPLINE
UPON A BROTHER

November 6, 1988

During the months of September and October 1988 we had much consideration with all the elders in Anaheim regarding how to handle the problem of a certain brother and what action should be taken. It was a matter of serious misconduct on the part of the brother, and due to the ramifications of the affair Godfred, Al, and I, who were more familiar with the case, felt that church discipline should be exercised. Minoru and Philip, the other two elders, did not agree but said they would not try to stop this being done.

The date was eventually set for the Lord's Day, November 6th. Minoru and Philip still dissented from the decision, but Godfred, Al, and I due to the serious nature of the problem, felt that we must go ahead to deal with it on the English-speaking side even without unanimity with the other two brothers on the Chinese-speaking side. The two brothers agreed to read our statements in the Chinese-speaking meeting, and then follow it with statements of their own dissenting from the action and explaining why. In the English-speaking side we would make our statement and follow it by reading the statements of Minoru and Philip.

Thus, at the end of the Lord's Day meeting, November 6th, Godfred stood and asked all the saints to read 1 Corinthians 5:6-11. He then said that in obedience to the Word of God we must ask all the saints not to associate with the brother being disciplined since we had sufficient evidence that he was such a one as described in 1 Corinthians 5:11.

He then read statements by Minoru and Philip dissenting from the announcement. Of course it was a highly unusual step to take without the consensus of the brothers and indeed regrettable that all the elders could not concur in this matter. By this you may realize the situation among the elders and realize how strongly we felt about the matter.

After the meeting, Godfred and I visited the wife of the disciplined brother and told her that this action did not apply to her or her children. She had come to the meeting in defiance of Godfred asking her not to come. She was greatly grieved, and we felt sorry for her.

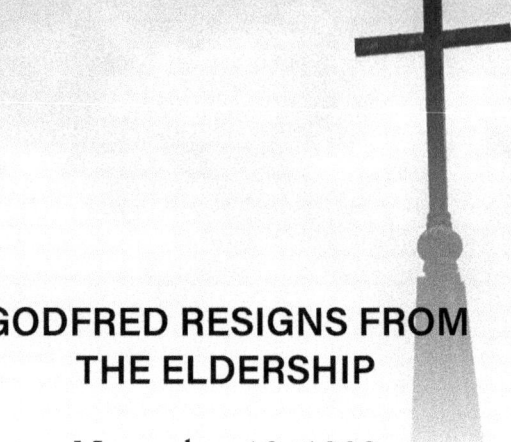

GODFRED RESIGNS FROM THE ELDERSHIP

November 13, 1988

Early this year (1988), Godfred informed Al and me that due to the impossibilities of the present church situation as he saw them, he was seriously considering to withdraw from the eldership. We were shocked. I strongly urged him not to do that but to continue with us for some time until we see how things would turn out. We desperately needed his help. To our great relief he assented to do that.

On September 30th, Godfred again informed Al and me that this time he definitely intended to resign from the eldership and that the next day he would go to Brother Lee to notify him of his decision. He felt that due to all his complications in Anaheim it was impossible to have a church. But he indicated that he would remain with us in the eldership a little longer until the problem related to the brother whom we disciplined was resolved. Thus, when the disciplinary action was taken on November 6th, Godfred informed us that he would promptly resign the following Lord's Day and would announce it to the saints.

On the Lord's Day morning, November 13th, I communicated with Godfred before the meeting, hoping at the last moment to forestall his resignation. I urged him to delay a little longer so that eventually, if the Lord should lead, we could all resign together. It seemed better to me that it would be better for us to act together. But he felt definitely and strongly that he must take this step. His course was set, and he could not be turned aside.

We had good fellowship in the meeting over Ephesians 4:17-32. At the close Godfred stood as planned and announced that he was resigning as an elder in the church in Anaheim, saying that it was a matter of conscience. The elders of the churches, he said, were expected to carry out Brother Lee's burden and he could not conscientiously do that because of various practices and teachings that had come in. It was an exceedingly short statement, but it caused quite a stir. After the meeting about a dozen saints gathered around him and plied him with many questions and concerns. He lingered there in the meeting hall and conversed with them till nearly 2:00 P.M. Many saints had a high esteem for Godfred and his function and were wondering what would happen now that he was leaving. Al and I also wondered what we would do at this juncture. We felt we had no alternative but to remain, at least for some time, in the eldership.

TENSE CONVERSATIONS AND STRAINED RELATIONSHIPS WITH A GROUP OF ANAHEIM SAINTS

December 1988 – February 1989

On December 20, 1988, after the church prayer meeting, a letter dated December 16, 1988, was handed to us by Daniel Sun, a brother in Anaheim, addressed to the elders and signed by eleven saints in the church including both brothers and sisters. After referring to the meeting of October 27th when we met with some of them, the letter said, "In view of what has developed, we feel the need for further fellowship and request that you meet with us as soon as possible due to the urgency of the issues." The letter then addressed seven areas of their concern. Because these concerns expressed the feelings of a number of saints in Anaheim, we will record them here in an abridged form. For the convenience of the reader, we will also include our response in an abridged form under each item.

1. Distribution of transcripts of the meeting on August 28, 1988 (sixteen points given by Godfred and me and confirmed in testimony by Al). They desired us to denounce this distribution openly before the saints and also to write an open letter to other churches to denounce the same. They further requested that we clarify that those points did not represent the feelings of all the elders or of all the saints, specifically those who signed this letter.

Response: We feel that the distribution of the sixteen points was allowed sovereignly by the Lord and used by Him. The points are solidly based on the Word of God and are for the greater part what we have always believed and taught in the Lord's recovery since the beginning. Therefore, we do not feel that we can or should denounce their distribution either by word or by letter. Of course, some of the points were especially suited to our local situation and should be viewed as such. It is clear from the transcript that we did not purport to represent all the saints or all the elders. Should any saints have difficulties with these points, we encourage them to indicate their difficulties specifically in writing and send them to us; we will be happy then to address them in further fellowship.

2. The distribution of the flyer entitled Significant Dates in the History of the Church in Anaheim (in English and Chinese). They asked us to publicly denounce the distribution of the flyer and to rebuke those who were responsible for it in order to stop such lawlessness.

Response: We feel it is wholly out-of-character and unbecoming to Christians to distribute such a flyer anywhere. We hope it will not be distributed in our meeting hall or in any place where the saints gather.

3. Untrue statements, public accusations, and character assassinations. They said that many untrue statements had been made during recent meetings which should be corrected and dealt with by the elders. Moreover, they said that many public accusations had been made in the last few months which had grieved and offended many saints. They felt that the elders should help those who spoke these to deal with their offenses.

Response: Concerning some of the statements deemed offensive and untrue, Godfred has already publicly denounced and rebuked these. We encourage the saints offended by other matters shared to go directly to the brothers themselves according to the Lord's teaching in Matthew 18. We have spoken privately to a number of saints whose speaking may have been offensive, advising them to consider before the Lord what action He would have them to take.

4. Our relationship with Brother Lee. They felt that since the church had a long and close relationship with him, and since many saints consider him as the Lord's servant and would like to continue to receive help,

the elders should be fair to all the saints and allow the same freedom of close fellowship between the church and him.

Response: We acknowledge the long and close relationship with Brother Lee and desire to be fair to all the saints. Our attitude is that we would like to practice true generality, where all the saints are free to follow their own conscience. Any saints desiring to receive Brother Lee's ministry by attending trainings and conferences or reading his books are at full liberty to do so. If any prefer not to do this, we should also afford them this liberty.

5. Brother Joseph Fung's visit to Anaheim. They felt that the presence of this brother at this time was not profitable to the church since he associates himself, they said, with many of the saints opposing Brother Lee's ministry and has made many slanderous and divisive statements.

Response: Whether or not Joseph's presence here is profitable for the church, only the Lord knows and can judge. We do not have any jurisdiction to ask him to leave the area. In fact, we consider that his visit has been helpful to many saints, and that our fellowship with him has been constructive for the building up of the church.

6. Regarding discipline exercised upon a certain brother. They did not agree with any decision issuing from an eldership that was not unanimous.

Response: Of course, it was a highly unusual step to take without the consensus of the brothers and indeed regrettable that all the elders could not concur in this matter. By this you may realize the situation among the elders and how strongly we felt about the matter.

7. How do we go on? Regarding this point they said, "We feel we do love Christ and the church. We need to go on not only for a few saints but for many. We need your fellowship in this area."

Response: We answered this question under four headings:

a) By receiving the Word of God. Our greatest need is for the Lord to speak to us through His Word. Without the Lord's speaking it is impossible to go on or have a proper church life. The best way to overcome many troubling factors is to be well-nourished by the living, spoken Word of God. Our church life and daily life should be governed in all things solely by the Word of God, not by any expediency, tradition, or extraneous influence.

b) By following the Spirit's leading. In order to do this, we must give the Lord His rightful place as our unique Head. As the church and as individuals we are directly responsible and accountable to the Lord, and we need to receive our leading in all things from Him Who is now the Spirit within us. In order to seek the Lord's leading, we need much more earnest prayer than we now have.

c) By practicing and keeping the oneness of the Spirit. To do this we must learn to receive all whom God receives with the love and grace of Christ regardless of their concepts or convictions. We hope that we will come out of any party or sectarian oneness that excludes other members. Moreover, we must learn to practice the proper generality in our attitude toward one another. In Anaheim at the present time, we have the best environment to practice this generality that we have so long been taught but very little lived.

d) By preaching the gospel to the unbelievers and shepherding the saints. We sincerely hope that the Lord will raise up a healthy, normal, daily gospel preaching among us; this is vital to our going on. We hope that we may have a happy church life as a strong base and impetus for the spread of the gospel. With the gospel preaching we need adequate shepherding of all the new believers with the best use of home gatherings, either in their homes or in the homes of the saints.

After receiving the letter from these three brothers, we began to consider how best to respond. After much consideration we felt that due to the serious nature of the matters raised and demands made, we would answer the signatories of the letter in writing. Furthermore, due to the fact that many saints (not only the signatories of the letter) held concerns about the same matters, we decided to distribute copies of our response to all the saints that they may know where we stood on these matters. In the response distributed to all the saints we deleted our reply to item #6 since that touched upon a highly personal and sensitive matter. We include the full text of our response distributed to all the saints in the Appendix (see page 89, Appendix C). We also decided to append to the response an edited copy of the sixteen points given on August 28th so that they may have it for their reference, since it was referred to several times in the response.

We distributed the response to the signatories of the letter on Saturday evening, January 7th, and after the Lord's Day morning meeting, January 8th, we gave out an amended copy of the response (as mentioned above) to all the saints. Some of the brothers who had signed the letter to us were very unhappy that we made such a distribution to the saints; so we promised to meet with them the following evening to talk about the matters.

On Monday evening, January 9th, 1989, we met then with the brothers who had signed the letter to us. On February 7th, about one month later, we met with them again. During those times the brothers grilled us and accused us in a manner that was quite out-of-character for them. This led us to suspect that they were receiving direction from behind the scenes. (We received a definite report through one of them to another brother that they had met with Brother Lee and talked with him about the Anaheim elders.) The atmosphere in these meetings was tense and oppressive. We felt that it was altogether not profitable for anyone or for the whole situation to meet in such a way. The chief spokesman for the brothers said to my face bluntly, emphatically, and with great finality, "We will not follow your direction!" Minoru Chen, one of the other elders in Anaheim, strongly confirmed and supported them. The meetings succeeded only in letting us know how they felt about some things, matters which we held an altogether different view and told them so.

These brothers, with two or three exceptions, had been with us for many years and knew us well, as we did them. Most all of them were exceedingly quiet and retiring brothers, but they represented a number of saints who desired to receive Brother Lee's ministry and leadership and were not happy with the way we were taking, although we endeavored to practice generality toward all saints regardless of their preference. They obviously did not agree with that or appreciate that. It was abundantly clear that, at least to them, our eldership was in name only. It was a grievous situation and one that could not continue much longer.

ELDERS FROM THE CHURCH IN RALEIGH, N.C. VISIT BROTHER LEE

January 1989

I include in this narrative a brief account of the visit of the Raleigh brothers to Brother Lee, as related to me by them, since it affords another window upon the actual situation and since Brother Lee asked the Raleigh brothers to convey some concerns and questions to the elders in Anaheim.

In the summer of 1988, Tom Cesar of the church in Raleigh came to Anaheim to discuss with Brother Lee the points of a seventy-one-page compendium entitled Concerns with our Practice Regarding Truth and Life, which had been mailed to him earlier. The brothers in Raleigh had labored for many hours over this work in the expectation that Brother Lee would read it, be apprised of their concerns, realize the gravity of the situation, and hopefully make some major changes in the course we were taking. Under each point they had put together zeroxed copies of pages with quotes from Watchman Nee and Brother Lee's earlier printed ministry together with quotes from his recent ministry to prove that there had been significant changes contradicting Brother Lee's own teaching. While Tom was in Anaheim that summer I saw him, and learning that he had presented Brother Lee with this writing I commented, "I doubt that Brother Lee will read it. He doesn't like to read things of that nature, that raise questions concerning his work or ministry."

In the early fall of 1988 Brother Lee wrote to the brothers in Raleigh saying that he desired to meet with them face to face and clear up their concerns point by point. Later in December of that year he telephoned and asked them to come to Irving, Texas for the elders' meetings, and he would meet with them there. The Raleigh brothers were not free to come to Irving, so they agreed to come instead to Anaheim the week after the training to meet with Brother Lee. He said he would answer their questions.

They arrived on Saturday, January 7, and met with Brother Lee that night. They met also on the Lord's Day morning, afternoon, and evening, and again on Monday morning – a total of approximately ten hours. The first evening Brother Lee did most of the speaking, giving them a history of the "conspiracy and rebellion." However, the brothers were able to say a few things. Tom pointed out how the church life was going down, and they were looking for answers. He said they had no problem with the matters of the new way, but how it was carried out was a problem. They were not concerned for right and wrong, but for God's righteousness. They read some verses to him and quoted from the Normal Christian Church Life by W. Nee, but Brother Lee did not want to hear it. He said that he knew what Watchman Nee meant in that book, and what Watchman Nee meant then does not apply to today's situation. He said, moreover, that there is no basic problem among us, but only a storm in Germany and Anaheim. John So, he said, exercises a strong control over Stuttgart, and just like Bill Freeman (a former elder of the church in Seattle) he is trying to set up another ministry. One of the Raleigh brothers then asked how you can identify another ministry. Brother Lee replied that it is very difficult.

The brothers said that Brother Lee was very defensive at times and was like a ball bouncing from one matter to another. Tom Cesar asked, "Why can't brothers come together to discuss their concerns without being considered to be conspiring? " But Brother Lee, they said, had no ear to hear them. It was as if they were talking to the wall. He didn't want to clear up their points; he hadn't even read the outline they had presented to him the previous summer. He would not answer their questions directly. They were impressed that he never asked how the saints in the church in Raleigh were doing, as if he was not concerned for them. The brothers were very disappointed.

Brother Lee asked Tom Cesar to be his mediator and to convey four points of concern he had to Brother Al Knoch and me, which he did. I present them here with my answers:

1. Brother Lee has had a unique relationship with the church in Anaheim over the years, and now he has been excluded by the brothers.

Answer: We did not exclude him. Rather, we met with him repeatedly hoping that various problems could be resolved and eliminated so that we could go on together in a normal relationship. The fact is, Brother Lee stayed away from the meetings in Anaheim of his own choice for at least two years before we were awakened to the problems and opened to him about them. We wondered why he never came. He said publicly before a large assembly of elders at that time that he "lost interest in the church in Anaheim."

2. Why in the past fourteen months have the elders in Anaheim not invited Brother Lee to speak in the church?

Answer: Why did Brother Lee not come to the church meetings? Every Lord's Day we got into the Word, and there was opportunity for everyone to speak. We were not burdened to invite him to hold a conference or give some special messages. We did not feel the church had need of that.

3. Why did the Anaheim brothers not share the sixteen points with him before the meeting of August 28, 1988?

Answer: After all our previous fellowship with Brother Lee, we did not feel it would be useful or profitable to do that.

4. Why did John Ingalls drop the matter of having a meeting with Brother Lee and some brothers to study together the concerns that have been raised?

Answer: I have already answered this question. See pages 31-33. Brother Lee also told the Raleigh brothers that John Ingalls has the concept that Witness Lee is a king, and John is trying to raise himself up to that level. (The Lord knows all our hearts and will judge.)

BROTHER LEE'S REMARKS AT A CONFERENCE IN SAN DIEGO

January 1989

On the weekend of January 27-29, 1989, Brother Lee had a conference in San Diego. He believed he had discerned the reason why some of the older elders and coworkers had some concerns regarding his work and the local churches, and he enunciated his feelings in one of the conference meetings. He spoke as follows:

"So today, let me tell you, the problem among us is this: there is a kind of consideration among the older co-workers -- not all, but some. There was a kind of consideration -- Where shall they be? Brother Lee was the one who brought the recovery to this country and was the one who through the Lord's ministry brought many, many of the older co-workers into the recovery. But now this one who brought the recovery to this country is seemingly deviating. Deviating from what? Into what? That's right, deviating from the old into the new. Now some of the coworkers have to consider where they should be. Shall they remain in the old, or shall they go forth into the new? Go forth? To say this is easy. You have to pay a price, especially the older ones. They have made a success in the recovery according to the old way, but now the old way was annulled. Then what shall we do? If you were them, surely you would consider. I must tell you, this is the root of all the troubles among us today. All the other things are on the surface; the root is here. Now you know."

This analysis absolutely missed the mark. I was surprised when I read the transcript that he could judge so superficially by saying that the root of all the problems is that the older co-workers would not leave the old way and take the new. At the present time he has revised his explanation, yet still misjudges. He went on to speak of himself as follows:

"When I was told that I had deviated from the recovery, I checked with myself. Where? Where could I find my deviation? I couldn't find [anything]. So I could not have anything to repent of. I'm not proud. I'm sincere. I'm honest. I'm open. To tell you the truth, I like to repent. I have repented to the saints openly at least two or three times. Right? I didn't deviate from the recovery; rather I got into it more deeply. Right?

"I was in the Lord's interests exactly sixty years. Right? I surely, humbly tell you, I know what I'm doing. Especially a man at this age would not do anything in haste, not knowing what he is doing. I got attacked – you all know this. Right? I like to suffer, because I like to suffer for what I'm doing. I know."

"Dear saints, you have to realize that what we all have seen in the past is just some kind of organizational things. It was not organic. Right? I do not mean that there was absolutely nothing at all organic -- I would not say that. There were some parts organic, but the main situation was not organic. Could you follow me? And today what the Lord wants is to have a main item. The main item must be organic."

I record these remarks here because they manifest how Brother Lee felt about us at the time, and how he felt about himself and his work. The reader may make his own judgment from Brother Lee's words.

AN UNPRECENDENTED ANNUAL BUSINESS MEETING OF THE CHURCH IN ANAHEIM

March 5, 1989

The church in Anaheim was registered with the state of California as a non-profit religious corporation, and according to its by-laws must hold an annual business meeting of all the members (consisting of all those who were regenerated and expressed their intention to meet with the church in Anaheim) with the main purpose of electing directors of the corporation. Each year this matter was held speedily at the close of the Lord's Table meeting on the first Lord's Day of March. The directors, according to our practice, were always elders though not required by law to be elders – any bona-fide member could be nominated and elected. The election was held by a voice vote of all the members present with usually none dissenting, and the meeting was adjourned, the whole affair lasting not more than five minutes. I, believe many of the local churches are familiar with this practice. The saints were told and all realized that the church was not a secular entity to be administered as a business corporation in a worldly way, but since it owned property and received tax exemption it must in obligation to the State perform these legal functions however minimized they may be. Therefore, we endeavored to dispense with them as quickly as possible.

There were three directors who, according to the by-laws, served a three-year term on a rotational basis, meaning that every year one of the directors terms expired, and he must be either re-elected or replaced at the annual business meeting. The custom was to re-elect the one whose term expired, and it was always accomplished without any problem. Minoru Chen, Al Knoch, and myself were the directors. The one whose term expired that year was Minoru Chen, a brother who was transferred by Brother Lee from the church in Huntington Beach and appointed an elder in the church in Anaheim in March 1986. Most of the saints were aware that it was he whose term expired and that he must be considered for re-election. Now the problem to a number of saints was that he was an elder who stood strongly for Brother Lee's leadership, whereas those saints did not, and they would like to see him replaced. The rest of the saints desperately desired to see Minoru in that position. Such an abnormal and divided condition we had never experienced before.

The business meeting and election were to take place on the Lord's Day, March 5th. On Thursday evening, March 2nd, Al and I met with Minoru Chen and Philip Lin to discuss the agenda for the business meeting. Minoru made a point very strongly that according to our custom the directors should always be elders. In fact, without our knowledge, in the preceding Lord's Day meeting on the Chinese-speaking side, Minoru had educated the saints to this effect, pointing out that in the coming election for directors, they should do the same on the English-speaking side. This we declined to do in the present divided situation, since the by-laws expressly stated that any member of the corporation could be nominated and elected to the post. We anticipated that this time we would have to vote by ballot as there would likely be more than one candidate nominated.

As the day drew near, we learned there was much activity in progress to get out the vote, one side wanting to maintain Minoru in office as a director and the other wanting to replace him. The phone lines were hot. It was quite unseemly to say the least. Many saints were informed that they must show up in order to vote. If Minoru was voted out and replaced by someone who was not absolute for Brother Lee's leadership, that for some saints forebode an extremely unstable situation for the church and the property. If Minoru was elected that to some saints meant a foothold for Brother Lee and the LSM. We, speaking for Al and me, did not have any taste for the whole affair and were certain that in any case Minoru would be re-elected. If Al and I had wanted to remove Minoru (as some were charging us), since we constituted the majority of directors (two against one), we could, according to the by-laws, call a director's meeting and vote Minoru out of the directorship. But this we would never do.

At the close of the morning meeting on March 5th, the Chinese saints from their meeting on the other side of the building filed in, making a total of close to three hundred in attendance. As the president of the corporation, I was responsible to preside over the meeting. I stood and made a few introductory remarks concerning the nature of the meeting: I explained again that as a corporation we were bound legally to have the meeting and that it was a business meeting governed by by-laws, not a church meeting where anyone was free to speak as he was moved. The meeting was then called to order, the purpose of electing a director stated, and the meeting opened for nominations from the members. I endeavored to direct the meeting very strictly according to parliamentary procedure and the by-laws, to assure order, not give any ground for accusations, and eliminate any kind of maneuvering and disturbing behavior. It went fairly well considering the situation.

After a flurry of nominations, a number of which were declined, two persons remained to be voted upon: Chris Leu, who was not an elder, and Minoru Chen. Cards to serve as ballots were distributed, and four brothers chosen previously by the elders collected them and counted the vote. I myself abstained from voting. Minoru was elected, receiving 195 votes, to Chris Leu's 69. It was as I expected. When the count was announced by Al Knoch, the secretary of the corporation, many saints applauded with clapping of hands for Minoru's election. The meeting was soon adjourned.

I determined after that morning that I would never preside over such a church business meeting again. Such a function is wholly out of character with the church and utterly distasteful to the spirit. I was thoroughly fed up with the whole affair. It has been said that since I failed through the election to have someone else installed to replace Minoru, for that reason I resigned from the eldership. The Lord knows that this is far from the truth and is the product of someone's overworked imagination.

ALBERT KNOCH AND JOHN INGALLS RESIGN FROM ELDERSHIP

March 19, 1989

On Tuesday, March 14, 1989, Godfred, Al, and I had fellowship and prayer during the morning and then lunch together. It was a memorable time, a decisive time. I expressed strongly to the brothers my feeling concerning the futility and dishonesty of playing the role of elder in Anaheim any longer. It was hypocritical to go on in that status feeling as we did with strong conviction that we were in a system. Moreover, we were totally incapable of changing the course of the church or of practicing a generality with the saints where all were free to follow their own conscience. These considerations dictated that we should resign. Both Godfred and Al agreed. Of course, Godfred had already resigned and withdrawn from the eldership on November 13, 1988, about four months earlier, but he was still concerned for Al and me. We fellowshipped about this matter and felt very clear that we should take the step and resign. I proposed that we wait to announce this to the saints until I would return from a trip to Europe planned for the end of March, but both Godfred and Al urged that we should do it immediately. We decided then to make a statement to this effect in the coming Lord's Day morning meeting, giving the reasons for it.

This was a critical and momentous decision for us. I had been an elder in the church in Los Angeles for twelve years and in the church in Anaheim for fifteen years, during all this time closely associated with Brother Witness Lee. This decision would change the course of our lives and of the church, but we believed it was of the Lord.

On Friday evening, March 17th, Al and I met with the other elders, Minoru Chen and Philip Lin, and announced to them our intention to withdraw from the eldership, giving them some explanation. They received it and urged us to notify Brother Lee immediately. This we intended to do, and did so by letter the next day. Our letter is included in the Appendix (see page 93, Appendix D).

Thus, on the Lord's Day morning, March 19th, I rose at the close of the meeting and announced our decision to withdraw from the eldership of the church. I made a few introductory remarks, saying that "I began to realize that our practices have differed and deviated from our vision. Our vision was the same, our teaching was mostly the same, the truth is always the same, but our practice has really differed." I included a statement that the nature of what we called the Lord's recovery had changed, and then spoke in a number of points the reasons and basis for our decision to withdraw. I did this briefly without much elaboration, speaking for twenty-two minutes. I record here in abridged form the salient points. The full text is included in the Appendix (see page 94, Appendix E).

1. There has been a change in emphasis to the building up of the work or the ministry more than the local churches. The ministry has been promoted, exalted, and built up, and the churches have suffered greatly in the process.

2. There had been a great effort and promotion to unite the saints and the churches around a certain leader and organization.

3. There has been much pressure with full expectation that all the saints and the churches will conform to the burden of the ministry and be identical with one another in full uniformity of practice to carry it out.

4. In February 1986 we had signed a letter along with 417 other elders agreeing that we would be identical with all the churches, that we would follow the ministry absolutely, and that we realized Brother Lee's leading was indispensable to our oneness. Since these matters were not in agreement with the Word of God, we greatly regretted that we had subscribed to them, and I stated publicly that I would retract my signature.

5. There has been an emphasis, at least in practice, on a centralization of the churches and the work.

6. There has been a pervasive control exercised over the church, not so much directly, but very much indirectly, which makes it difficult to go on by getting our leading directly from the Lord.

7. Church history reveals that denominations have begun with the affiliation of groups of saints under one leadership followed by the commencement of a training center. We were also going that way.

8. I greatly appreciate Brother Lee's portion, but he has been exalted and honored above what is written, according to 1 Corinthians 4:6.

9. Brother Lee and his ministry have been made a great issue and factor of division among us.

10. Our going on and our relationship with the saints and with the church is made to depend on our relationship with Brother Lee. When this is done the ground of oneness is replaced with something else.

11. We have applied the teaching concerning the ground of oneness in a divisive and sectarian way, so that we divide ourselves from other Christians. This is due to an improper attitude and application of the truth. In the local churches we have become narrow and small as manifested in our attitude toward other Christians and in our reception of other saints.

12. Our attitude toward other Christians is one of belittling them and thinking we're superior. What we need is the reality of oneness, not just the teaching or slogan.

13. The Lord told us in His Word to go forth to Him outside the camp. The Lord is still calling His sheep out of every fold and every camp so that there can be one flock with one shepherd.

14. Our oneness should be as large as the whole Body of Christ. Any oneness that is smaller than this we should leave and not keep.

15. We should all go directly to the Lord for His leading in the church in order to have a local administration, at the same time maintaining

a proper fellowship with other saints and other churches. At this point I quoted some sentences from a pamphlet entitled The Beliefs and Practices of the Local Church, published by the Living Stream Ministry. One sentence reads: "In all administrative affairs, the local churches are autonomous and locally governed."

16. There has been an over-stressing and distortion of the teaching concerning deputy authority, which has caused the saints to be fearful to follow their conscience, to be one with their spirit, and sometimes to speak their genuine concerns.

17. There has been too much emphasizing of methods more than the inner anointing, and external big success more than the experience of the inner life.

18. We have no problem with the matters of the "new way". We wanted to make that clear. Actually, these things are not new.

In conclusion I said, "Based on the above points, we feel we must withdraw from the eldership. We are not able to lead you in this way, nor are we able to lead you out of this way. Many of you feel strongly that you would like to take a certain direction, and as elders we cannot lead you in that direction…. We really love you in the Lord. The Lord knows that. We care for you, and we wish you all the very best in the Lord. You are in our prayers. You will always be in our prayers. We ask you to pray for us too. Pray for Brother Al and me. If we've offended any of you saints, we ask you to please forgive us. We surely never intended to offend any one of you. We still like to keep our fellowship with you all as fellow-members of the Body of Christ."

Al Knoch then rose and spoke for eleven minutes, giving a very genuine and touching statement regarding his inner feeling about the eldership. I will just quote briefly here. He began: "I am so thankful that John could share those points, because I could not do it so clearly. I hold the same concerns…. These were the same concerns we presented to Brother Lee in all our times with him. So he knows all of these things already, and he has considered them….As elders in the recovery we do have a problem with many of our practices, and there's no way we could in a good conscience continue on in the position without the reality. How can we lead you? We can't lead in that way, and yet the recovery is going that way.

"So we brothers feel…it's good for us, it's good for you, and it's good for the Lord that we withdraw at this time. The reason we didn't withdraw sooner, though we were clear to withdraw last December, is that we felt the need to stand here for these very concerns for a while longer to see what could be done, and to see how the saints would respond to this kind of stand. But the more we have done this, the more clear we have become that there will not be any change at this time in the way the recovery is going."

The saints, generally speaking, listened well, only interrupting once. The Lord's presence and strengthening were with us. Minoru Chen closed the meeting, saying that we all must realize that the points I had made were an expression of my own personal view. He made a special point of controverting my assertion that the nature of the recovery had changed. He said that the nature of the recovery had indeed not changed. That was his view.

I also resigned by letter from the board of directors and the presidency of the corporation. A great step had been taken and a turn made. The next day I left with my wife for Europe, where I rested, while visiting and fellowshipping with a number of churches. Upon returning to Anaheim on May 2nd I was not led of the Lord to return to the meetings on Ball Road, where I had met with the saints for fifteen years, and where I had resigned from the eldership on March 19th. I continued to gather with saints for the Lord's Table in one of the couple's homes, where I had been meeting for some time prior to resigning.

NEW ELDERS APPOINTED TO REPLACE KNOCH AND INGALLS

April 2, 1989

On the Lord's Day, April 2nd, at the end of the meeting, Minoru Chen stood and read a letter addressed to the saints from Brother Lee in Taiwan, appointing two brothers to replace Al and me in the eldership. They were Eugene Gruhler, who was brought from Denver, and Francis Ball, who was transferred from San Gabriel. These brothers had been elders in Anaheim some years previously. They were both present in the meeting as Minoru read Brother Lee's letter. The full text of the letter is included in the Appendix (see page 100, Appendix F).

In the letter, Brother Lee acknowledged that he had received our letter notifying him of our resignation, and had also heard of its accomplishment. He remarked, "I am very sorry for the two brothers that their course in following the Lord would have such an issue." He went on to say that he was very much concerned for the eldership in the church in Anaheim, and that he had felt led of the Lord to ask Eugene Gruhler and Francis Ball to "reassume their eldership in Anaheim in meeting the urgent need there...." Later in the year we heard that six more elders had been appointed by Brother Lee to the eldership in Anaheim, making a total of ten. Thus, our eldership had been replaced, revised, and greatly enlarged in number.

CONCLUSION

We have been deeply burdened that many saints who have been associated with the local churches may know the facts concerning events that transpired in these recent years and have a clear view of the whole situation. To facilitate this, we have recorded and published for the sake of history and for the readers' benefit this somewhat detailed but accurate account of what actually happened during the two years, 1987 to 1989, when our conscience was much exercised over the present situation and we responded as we felt appropriate and necessary. We cannot agree that the Lord's people should only hear from one source and be given, to say the least, a distorted and, in many particulars, an untrue account of our history and intention, as has been done recently. Therefore, with much consideration and heart searching and with many prayers we have published this account that the reader himself may judge from the facts and our intentions and come to a settled conviction before the Lord.

It is not our desire, nor has it ever been, to overthrow anyone's work or ministry, neither have we desired to put anyone's ministry aside, but rather to bring everything to the light and put everything in the proper context. A report has been circulated that we would not be satisfied until we brought a certain person down; this report was erroneously applied to us. We never had any such intention, nor have we ever conspired against anyone – the Lord knows this and can testify for us. The accusation of conspiracy made against us is an utter falsehood – our testimony as recorded in this account bears this out. Rather we have grieved over those in leadership who have swerved from the path they once proclaimed and espoused. We desperately hoped there would be some change to resolve the serious problems that had emerged, and we fellowshipped earnestly with Brother Lee to this end (see pages 19 -22 and elsewhere). We have lamented the damage inflicted and suffered by many saints through practices and attitudes that we, too, in some measure participated in while in that system from which we have come out. For my part I humbly repent for this.

We are also widely and vociferously accused of being rebellious and of fermenting and fomenting rebellion. This also is an extremely serious charge, and one which I feel obliged to respond to and deny. Against whom, I would ask, are we rebelling? And what was our act of rebellion? For my part I have always sought to have a good conscience before God and man. To remain silent, I a situation of departure and degradation, or to withdraw into "judicious obscurity", as some have done, would have been for me unconscionable. Not to speak out or to refrain from warranted action would have been for me a form of rebellion against the Lord's inner speaking and urging. My object was to follow the Lord, obey His Word, and practice the truth, fearing only Him. Perhaps I feel short in some particulars. Apart from that however, "I am conscious of nothing against myself, yet I am not justified by this; but He who judges me is the Lord" (I Cor. 4:4).

I therefore consider the charge of rebellion to be totally inappropriate and unfounded. Is it rebellious to voice one's concerns, care for one's conscience, obey the Lord's Word, and follow the inner anointing? This is what I did and sought to do, as this account testifies. Was I ambitious for position or did I seek to raise a following for myself, as some say? The Lord knows that this is far from the truth. I can only consider the charges of rebellion and conspiracy to be a form of character assassination, and a means to cover one's own track.

A state of enormous confusion and misunderstanding exists at the present time due to the widespread distortion of the facts and our intentions. Therefore in publishing this record we have felt constrained to chronicle the events just as the Bible chronicles events, recounting both the good and the bad. When this is done everyone is inevitably exposed. The Lord does not let anyone off the hook. How good it is to be exposed that we may repent and not live the rest of our lives in darkness or error! We are very thankful to the Lord for His abundant mercy in enlightening our inner being, in disclosing our failures and errors of the past, and in giving us a new beginning. May He do the same for every reader. We pray that He will use this account to that end.

We invite enquiries and are open to further fellowship with those who are seeking the truth and the way to go on these days.

Note: We have also included in our Appendix an open letter to the saints in San Diego from John H. Smith of San Diego (See Appendix G, page 101), and an open letter written by Albert Zehr of Burnaby, B.C., Canada (See Appendix H, page 107). We urge the reader to peruse them.

OUR WAY FOR THE FUTURE

I am burdened now to share some of my observations and inner exercises for our going on and our future. We should not remain in limbo or in spiritual no-man's land, but go on to satisfy the Lord and fulfill our calling. One has said that the greatest thing we learn from history is that we don't learn from history, and thus we are destined to repeat it. May the Lord be merciful to us that we may break out of that well-trodden path. We have spent countless hours analyzing not only our past but our inner being as well to discover by the Lord's mercy where we have missed the way and how we should return to Him and walk in His light and truth. Surely, we have very much to learn. Having invested our lives, our families, and our futures for decades in a way which at the beginning held so much promise, and then seeing it eventually turned aside and in a state of departure, how much we need the Lord's grace so that all we have experienced and passed through may not be in vain! We need His mercy that we may learn some precious lessons and not repeat history, but rather go on to satisfy Him and fulfill His purpose before His coming!

Our greatest indictment, undoubtedly, is that we have been away from the Lord. Hence, our urgent need in these days is to return to the Lord Himself, to focus on Him, and to care supremely for our relationship with Him. Even more than attempting to correct abuses and unbalances we need to center on our Lord Jesus and pursue after Him. This has been the greatest lesson the Lord is seeking to teach me. To those who were caught in a religious system while He was on the earth Jesus said, "Come to Me!" That was His central call, and He voiced it again and again. He surely exposed the system and spoke scathing rebukes to its leaders, but He also gave those with an ear a door out and a very positive direction: "Come to Me!" "Come to Me, all you who labor and are heavy laden, and I will give you rest" (Matt. 11:28). What a precious word for today! "Let us therefore go forth to Him outside the camp…." (Heb. 13:13). To come out and yet not pursue Him so that He becomes everything to us is indeed vanity. Then we simply fall into another camp, call what we may.

This is a day characterized by "the passing of the hero." It should be for us a day of the passing of all the heroes, of all those who rival the place of the Lord Himself. Isaiah said, "In the year that King Uzziah died, I saw the Lord sitting on a throne, high and lifted up" (Isa. 6:1). It is best for all the kings to "die" as far as we are concerned so that we may see the Lord Himself high and lifted up. To see Him in such a way has a mighty life-changing and life-compelling effect, as it did on Isaiah (see Isa. 6:5-8). Our problem is that when one king dies, we replace him with another. When one hero passes away, we find another hero that suits our taste. If it is not someone else, it may sometimes be ourself. May the Lord deliver us from any form of hero worship and bring us wholly back to Himself. This is surely a great lesson and a continual exercise.

On the mount of transfiguration, Peter saw with Jesus the two Old Testament heroes, Moses and Elijah, and would memorialize them along with Jesus. To Peter they were still heroes, as they were to all the Jews of his day. The Father then removed the heroes and pointed Peter to His Beloved Son. May He so the same for us. And "they saw on one except Jesus Himself alone" (Matt. 17:8). Strangely enough, after the Lord's death and resurrection, Peter himself was made a hero, along with Paul and Apollos, by the saints in Corinth, and the Lord had to speak again through His servant Paul to recover the saints to Himself. Paul said, "Neither is the one who plants anything nor the one who waters, but the One who makes to grow, God" (I Cor. 3:7). What a blessed day when we see no one but Jesus Himself alone! The Lord is indeed jealous of our affection and wants it all.

Fang Lizhi, the noted Chinese dissident and promoter of the current democracy movement in China made the following statement recently: "If the Chinese want a heroic person to tell them what to do and to lead them, I am not that man, because I think when people put such hopes and faith in a single leader, it is not only unhealthy but also dangerous." Although these words were not spoken in the realm of spiritual things, I consider them to be words of great wisdom and understanding and a most appropriate comment on the situation we have addressed. Oh, that all the Lord's people could be so clear!

This is not to say that we do not need proper leadership. The Word of God refers in a number of places in the New Testament to leaders among God's people. Hebrews 13:17 says, "Obey those who lead you and submit to the, for they watch over your souls as those who will give account...." The outstanding characteristic of true leaders, however, is that they lead not just by teaching, but much more by example. Peter said very pointedly that the elders should shepherd the flock, not seeking gain by base means or lording it over them, but becoming patterns of the flock. (I Pet. 5:2-3). Heb. 13:7 says concerning the leading ones that we should consider the issue of their manner of life and imitate their faith. Proper examples and patterns of the flock are sorely needed today. Paul said, "Be imitators of me, as I also am of Christ" (I Cor. 11:1)

In the light of recent scandals involving TV evangelists, reporters asked Billy Graham (who is now commendably as "Mr. Clean", since he has preserved a reputation untainted by improper conduct) how such despicable behavior as evidenced in current Christian leadership could be avoided I the future. Billy Graham responded with three notable points:

1. Make public the financial statements of your organization.

2. Do not have family members on your Board of Directors.

3. Practice what you preach.

The first two points are undoubtedly of signal importance and should be observed by every Christian organization, but I believe that the third, although somewhat of a cliché, is the greatest. We certainly would all subscribe to that; but how exposing that Christian leaders "Take heed to yourself [first] and to the teaching...for in doing this you will save both yourself and those who hear you" (I Tim. 4:16).

May we all freshly heed such counsel for ourselves. We have received seemingly endless teaching and have accumulated much knowledge, but we have stunted growth and corresponding practice.

What then shall we do? It is exceedingly clear to many that the Lord needs a new beginning. Throughout church history He has had many new beginnings, and it seems that the time has come for another. But how to go on is the great question. How can there be a new beginning where we live and where we are concerned? The greatest need, I believe, is a genuine and deep return to the Lord Himself in our personal and daily lives, and then a coming together with others of like vision, perhaps just one or two, to pray earnestly for His kingdom to come and His will to be done on earth where we are. The need of prayer at this time for the Lord's testimony in our lives and among His people is very great – prayer with "earnest insistence and resolute persistence", believing the Lord to answer our prayer for His will. The first and greatest effect of our prayer will be a renewing work in us.

We need a new beginning, I believe, in a very simple way, meeting together with a small number, as the Lord leads us, not in any sect or division, but seeking to keep the oneness of the Spirit that we may have a true expression of His one Body. It is a relief not to try to do a great work or to expect large numbers or to look for something to develop quickly according to our concept. I am very thankful for the Lord's word to the meager remnant struggling to have a new beginning in the Old Testament: "Not by might, or by power, but by My Spirit, says the Lord of hosts. Who are you, O great mountain? Before Zerubbabel you will become a plain; and he will bring forth the top stone with shouts of Grace, grace to it!...For who has despised the day of small things?" (Zech. 4:6-7,10). What a blessing to be in such a simple company to receive these words! For my part, I just want to be a brother among brothers, not in any special class, but focusing on Christ, loving Him, trusting Him, receiving the portion of others and sharing whatever I may have, caring for the saints, and rebuilding the Lord's house. I believe that such companies of saints, through they be small, will be very effective in bringing in His kingdom and testimony.

Certainly, we should still hold and seek to walk in all that the Lord Himself has shown us concerning Christ and His Body the church, at the same time seeking further light and adjustment where necessary. May the Lord save us from throwing out what is purely the truth; rather we should throw out the malpractice of the truth. Most of all we should throw out our self and deny our self. We need discernment with a sober mind to distinguish the things that differ. The truth itself should not be faulted or blamed or abandoned just because it has been abused or misused. Indeed, the truth may well need some clarifying (not changing), and our practice of it will certainly need adjusting. Let us hold the truth in love and seek to experience its reality. I believe that if we focus on Christ Himself and His living Word, many things will fall into place spontaneously, and we will have more reality and walk in it. How much we need this!

May we bring people to the Lord and to His pure Word, not opposing anything just because a certain person spoke that thing, or because that was something practiced in the past. I am afraid that if we focus on certain practices, whether old or new, and make issues of them, we will be distracted from the Lord Himself. This is what we did in the past. Of course, we should not be confined in any old mold, but seek to be truly free in the Spirit. The essential factor is not new or different methods (though we should be open to anything of the Lord), but the Spirit. We should not be shaken or distracted from our vision by anyone's malpractice. May the Lord grant us the grace to overcome all kinds of reactions and follow Him in the Spirit with others.

Thus, we need to return to the Lord Himself and to His Word. We have paid too much attention in the past to the interpretation of the Bible rather than to the Word of God itself. We have acquired much knowledge of the Word as it were from a second-hand store, relying excessively on the messages and writings of others, whereas we need to seek light and personal revelation from the Word for ourselves. This does not mean that we despise ministers of the Word who lead us by the Word to Him – we thank God for them. I am impressed that we need to pray much for the Lord's timely speaking to His people. There has been a shortage of the undeniable prophetic word that makes the mind of God for the present day known to His people. May the Lord have a further recovery of the genuine prophetic speaking, not merely touching on external events, but communicating and unveiling the will of God in spiritual reality so that His purpose may be accomplished among us and His kingdom come. Thank God there is some amount of this.

I believe many will agree that we also need a recovery of genuine love and care for the saints. They have suffered much and have been neglected. Many are scattered and wounded and seemingly forgotten, like the man going down from Jerusalem to Jericho who was robbed, stripped, beaten, and desperately needed a "neighbor" (Luke 10:25-37). That man typified the Lord's people. I pray that the Lord will transform many of us from lawyers to neighbors who minister much-needed help to the saints, and that He will raise up "inns" where these can be cared for.

The Lord undoubtedly desires to do a purifying work in us, not only removing any residue of bitterness we may have due to the past and every fleshly reaction, but giving us a single and pure heart for Himself and His testimony. To come out of a system is relatively easy, but to have so many fallen things removed from us requires the Lord's great mercy and deep work. I have deeply sensed my need for the Lord's purifying work, and have realized that the Lord can only have a new beginning by making us new.

There has been an intense spiritual warfare raging to destroy and then to oppose the recovering of the Lord's testimony. This is the intrinsic meaning, I believe, of all that we have passed through and are continuing to experience. It is illustrated by the destruction of Jerusalem (which had its root in the inner corrupting elements), and the al-out opposition to the building of the walls of Jerusalem, as seen I the book of Nehemiah. I believe we are in that stage now, when there is resistance and antagonism, both violent and subtle, from without and from within, to the raising up of the Lord's testimony. The present situation surely requires some with the spirit and heart of Nehemiah, willing to lay down their lives for the Lord's purpose, and not wanting anything for themselves; not fighting with the arm of flesh, but standing unshaken in the Lord, watching and praying. "For our struggle is not against flesh and blood." To react in any way in our flesh, or to dwell forever on the past, licking our wounds, accomplishes the enemy's designs as well as any other deception, for the Lord still does not get His testimony. May the Lord give us intelligence in the spiritual warfare that we may go on very positively to provide Him with His heart's desire, His dwelling place. May He shepherd His sheep and gather them together. and may His great and exhaustless grace be with us all.

APPENDIX A

STATEMENTS, IMPRESSIONS AND QUOTES FROM FTTT

Statements and impressions that have disturbed 2-weekers and 6-weekers during the training in Taipei, and that have troubled others upon hearing them:

1. The prediction that the Lord is coming back in 13 years.

2. The talk of a global coordination, indicating that the elders and the churches should follow not only in principle, but also in detail, what comes out from Taipei. This global coordination was one of the goals of the recent gospel festival in Taipei. There was also talk that the brothers in various places should keep in touch with Andrew Yu regularly to keep up with the latest details.

3. All the brothers must go to Taipei to be brought into the oneness they have there.

4. If you have not gone to Taipei, you are not in the Lord's move.

5. A brother who was concerned for the saints in the church in Dallas was told by Benson to forget the saints and go out, knock on doors, and raise up a new church life. Eventually some of the older saints would then join him.

6. Gene Ford's recent message excessively exalting Brother Lee.

7. Jake Jacobson's statement that he had the "Witness Lee fever."

8. Many other people besides the Lord elevated, flattered, called heroes, and publicly given awards.

9. The trainers pounding upon the full timers for hours upon end to urge and incite them to remain in Taipei for another term.

A statement made by Paul Hon to Don Rutledge in July 1986, in Don's home in Dallas. (Witnesses present: Bill Lawson, Louis Chen, Tom McNaughton).

The following was spoken by Paul Hon in the context of how to be one with the ministry:

The Father is #1, the Son is #2, the Spirit is #3, and Witness Lee is #4; and then there are those with Witness Lee. Don Rutledge asked, Paul, who is #5. Paul replied that it is not yet clear who #5 is. Then Paul continued, You brothers don't have access to Brother Lee; Andrew Yu and I do. We can walk into Brother Lee's apartment any time and sit down to eat breakfast with him. The way to know what Brother Lee wants is to do is to be in contact with those who have access to him. They will tell you what he wants you to do. Don Rutledge asked, Isn't this a hierarchy and the exercise of control? Paul replied, No! Then Don asked, How then does this differ from what we've been condemning. Paul answered, If the local brothers would practice in this way to carry out their burden, it would be a hierarchy and control. But if this is practiced to carry out the ministry's burden, it is not hierarchy or control.

Quotes from various sources:

"Since Christianity is in ruins, the Lord raised up the recovery; since the recovery is in ruins, the Lord raised up the FTTT." (Andrew Yu, Oct.,1987)

"Whatever Witness Lee says, we make it happen!" (Paul Hon in training).

"We're Witness Lee's Company." "I've got Witness Lee fever." (Jake Jacobson)

"There is no need to pray about what to do; just follow the ministry." (By the Trainers in Taipei)

"We don't even need to think; we just do what we are told." (Trainers)

"If the ministry says go east, you just go east. If the ministry says go west, you just go west." (Andrew Yu, The

Way To Go On, Voice of a High School Heart Newspaper, pg8) "Just give yourself to the ministry… that's all."

"No Opinions, no cold wind." (Trainers, FTTT)

Statements regarding leaving the training to return to one's own locality:

"If you leave the training, you'll miss the kingdom." (Trainers, FTTT) A strong implication that to return to your locality was to leave your first love for the Lord. This was stated to one trainee.

Statements regarding the oneness of the saints and churches with the ministry and the Living Stream Ministry Office:

"To be one with the ministry is to be one with Brother Lee, the office, and Philip Lee." (Not sure of who said this, but many similar statements have been heard)

"The office is Brother Lee." (Not sure of source)

"These things are being spoken in the highest echelons of the Lord's Recovery." (Jake Jacobson, Irving High School Training)

Regarding the Stadium Meetings in Taipei:

A mixture of the worldly elements with the fine flour:

Honor given to man: Nationalities stressed, various types of services honored, outstanding trainees awarded and honored.

Props: Flags, all kinds; bands, etc.,; marches; card section (as in American football rooting sections); audience applause.

These activities, culminating in the extreme events at the High School Training in Irving this summer, have caused many dear saints to feel that the nature of the Lord's Recovery is being changed.

APPENDIX B

THE PROPER STANDING OF THE CHURCH

From a meeting in Anaheim, California, August 28, 1988
Edited by John Ingalls and Albert Knoch.

Brother John Ingalls: We brothers do not like to be a mystery to you, and keep you wondering all the time, "Where do the brothers stand, and what are their feelings?" We feel that we owe you all some fellowship. We would like to share with you what should be our standing as a church according to the truth. Truth and confusion cannot go together.

Our standing is very important, even more important than our condition. When we have a clear, proper standing according to the truth in so many matters, this will properly affect our condition. You who have a family know how important the proper standing is: the husband has a certain standing; the wife has a different standing; and the children have yet another standing. Of course, in your job you had better be clear what is your standing, or you might get fired! Most importantly, as brothers and sisters in the church we must be clear what our standing is.

I hope that tonight we will all be cleared up. I also hope that by our fellowship you will realize that we are not against anyone, neither are we trying to put anyone down. Rather, we have the best interest of all saints upon our heart, and the best interests of the church. I also believe that we have the best interests of the Lord upon our heart. Saints, we are for you. And we believe that we are for the Lord and His recovery, for His truth.

1. First and foremost is, what is our standing in relation to the Word of God? This point must be first because it is very important, and all that we are going to share after this is solidly based in the Word of God. It is the truth. Saints, I believe we all agree that the Word of God should be our sole authority. This is our constitution. We read in the newspaper often how so many lawyers and congressmen are continually referring to the Constitution: "What does the Constitution say?" Saints, we all should be constantly referring to our constitution, the Word of God! I feel we need a reinstatement of the written Word of God as our sole authority. We want to be governed by the Word of God. I hope it could be true of us all that our consciences are bound by the Word of God; not by traditions, superstition, or anything else, but simply by the pure Word of the Lord. This Word must be our solid basis.

Also, I hope that we all would learn to test everything by God's Word, bringing everything to the light of the Word, even as the Bereans did in Acts 17:11. It says that they were more noble than those in Thessalonica because they received the Word with all eagerness, and then they searched the Scriptures to see if these things were so. The Lord commended them for doing this. The Bereans were searching out by the Scriptures the things which Paul was speaking. Now, Paul could have said to them: "Hey, wait a minute! Don't you know I am an apostle? How come you are looking into the Word about what I am speaking?" No, they checked him out by the Scriptures; and they were commended by the Lord as being noble for searching the Scriptures in this way. Saints, we all must do this, giving ourselves diligently to prove all things. God says in His Word to do this (I Thes. 5:21). The Word of God should be supreme among us; it must be our solid and sole basis.

2. Now, based upon the first point we go to the second, which is our standing concerning the church. From eternity, the church has been God's heart desire. He has set His heart upon this; the church is very precious to Him. Especially in this age in which we live, the church is central and supreme. No other corporate body is recognized by the New Testament in this age except the church. Everything is for the church; both the apostles, the ministry, and we all are for the church! All creation is for the church. God is working all things in this age for His church.

Furthermore, to take the proper standing as the church in each locality makes the church practical. Practically speaking, for us the church is local. The only proper standing we can see from God's Word is to stand upon the ground of the one Body in the locality where we live, to stand upon this precious ground of the oneness of the Body of Christ. I think this has been constituted into our being so that we could never, and we would never, give it up. I could never take any other standing.

We do not agree to be in any kind of sect, system, or division. We just like to be Christians – what we are by birth – standing upon the ground of the one Body of Christ, loving all Christians and being united with all Christians in Christ alone. We all have only one precious Head, and we re joined to Him as His one Body. This oneness is where all the blessings are, where so many precious things are! This which God has ordained in His Word should never be abandoned by us.

3. The third point is the genuine oneness: what should our standing and relationship be regarding this? First, we need a brief definition of what is the genuine oneness. Of course, this point goes right along with the church. This is also something most precious, because the Lord Jesus prayed for this:…that we all may be one, that we may be perfected into one (John 17:21-23). This very precious reality is our privilege to enjoy and partake of. Ephesians 4 calls this genuine oneness two things: the oneness of the Spirit, and the oneness of the faith. This oneness is something organic, not organized. It could never be organized, or taught; and, it cannot be forced. This oneness just needs to be kept, for it is the oneness of the Spirit. We have it in the Spirit with all saints; we just need to be diligent to keep it. How precious is this oneness! The Lord commands the blessing upon this (Psalm 133). It is a spiritual, organic oneness, which is totally in the realm of life and truth.

We must not build up any oneness that is outside the realm of life and truth, or we are liable to build up Babel. (Babel was a kind of oneness of the flesh, outside the realm of life and truth). The real oneness is of life. Actually, it is just Christ, Christ being enjoyed and experienced by us. When we are in the real enjoyment of Christ, we are enjoying the real oneness. Furthermore, this oneness is our testimony. The Lord Jesus prayed that we may be one, so that the world may know…Oh, this is powerful!

Of course, our standing in relation to this oneness is that our spirit could never agree with division of any kind. We do not like to be involved in any kind of division. We just like to keep the oneness of the Spirit in the uniting bond of peace. And, we like to arrive at the oneness of the faith which is common to all saints. Our saving faith is common to all believers. We desire to stand upon this oneness alone. All divisions either come out of sin, selfishness, or ambition; or, perhaps just ignorance. We must be enlightened to see that we should not be divided by anything. Spiritual leaders should never divide us. Nothing should divide us; rather, we should keep the genuine oneness of the Spirit, with all saints. Our oneness should be just as large in scope as the whole Body of Christ. Any oneness less than that we would not keep.

4. Our fourth point is along this same line: what is our standing in relation to other Christians? There are many other Christians besides us. To say nothing about the rest of the world, just here in Anaheim there must be thousands of other Christians. What is our standing in relation to all of them – and I include all who were once meeting with us, but who are no longer with us. They are all Christians. (They did not get unsaved!) Plainly speaking, our relationship to them should be that we love them all. We should love them all and receive them all, and feel that we really need them all.

Lately, I have been considering this matter: what does it mean to love others? I surely believe it is that we feel we need them. Oh, we need all other Christians! And we not only need them, we want them; and, we are very open to them, and we care for them. We just love them. Saints, I have been convicted by the Lord about my attitude toward other Christians, and I have been repenting of this. I feel that our attitude has not been the best: in the past, we have mocked and belittled other Christians. It is high time we stop this! We must have the proper attitude of love for all our brothers, for they are all members of the same Body. We are members one of another, so we must surely love all other members, including all who formerly met with us. Many who once met with us are still living right around us. But we have mostly just written them off. We feel, Forget about them. This is a wrong attitude. Recently a brother who left us ten years ago called on the telephone. I was so happy to hear from him. He was just reaching out for fellowship. Brother Al and I went to visit him, and we enjoyed the fellowship, and had good prayer. He loves the Lord, and is quite much for the Lord. I became very burdened to apologize for my attitude in the past; and, he forgave me. I appreciated that.

We must have the right attitude with the proper love for all saints, no matter where they are. This does not mean that we compromise the truth in any way. No, but we surely love all Christians. We should never think that we are better; we are probably worse than some. I am afraid that in the past – and I include myself – we have had an elitist attitude, thinking that we are some kind of spiritual elite. This is wrong. If our attitude is such, we are surely Laodicea – we are in a fallen state. Furthermore, what kind of practice is this among us of calling other saints negative? No! I'll tell you who is the only negative one: the devil. If you feel like calling someone negative, tell the devil, You are negative! We have called some saints negative, but actually, they only have some very genuine concerns. Why can't we believe that, and just love them? Oh saints, let us love all the members of the Body.

5. The fifth point is our standing in relation to our vocation. What is our work, our profession, our calling? In other words, what should we be doing? This question has been asked: What are we doing here, anyway? Saints, our vocation is just to build up the Body of Christ. This is our work, our profession, our service. Tonight, we sang in a hymn that nothing else shall suffice the Lord, but this. This is what He is doing today, building up His Body. And this is what the apostles exhorted us all to do. We all have a part in the building. First Corinthians 3 tells us that we all are building. Everyone is building upon the foundation which has been laid. This chapter also warns us to be careful how we build: we must use the proper materials. Ephesians 4 speaks about the work of the ministry unto the building up of the Body of Christ, and about the Body building itself up in love. So, saints, our work, our vocation, is to build up the Body, and be for the building up. We must not build up anything else.

When we speak about what our standing should be, we also must make clear what our standing should not be: it should not be to build up any work or ministry. In fact, all ministry must be for the Body. We sang tonight that all the ministry is for the churches, not the churches for the ministry. So, our vocation is to build up the Body. And it is here that we all have a lot to do, to build up one another in life and oneness, to build up the Body of Christ!

6. Our sixth point goes right along with this: what is our purpose, or aim? It is to be the Lord's testimony, His full expression. The Lord needs His expression on this earth today, so this should also be our aim. The end product must be that we have a testimony, and that we be His testimony. We are not here for a work or an activity. (I do not mean that we should not go and preach the gospel. Don't misunderstand me.) We are here simply to be His testimony.

I have recently been reading Nehemiah. This book shows Jerusalem's sad case: the walls were broken down and the gates burned with fire. Nehemiah saw this, and not only was his spirit stirred up, but his heart was very concerned and burdened. Jerusalem, the Lord's people, were in reproach. Saints, I honestly feel that we have been in reproach, with no testimony. The walls are broken down and the gates are burned with fire! The walls not only speak of separation, but also of the testimony. I hope that the Lord will recover us to build up the walls of Jerusalem, to build up His testimony. The Body needs to be built up so that we will be a testimony. Dear Lord, recover us! Recover your testimony! Saints, this must be our standing, that we just want to be the Lord's testimony.

7. The seventh point is, what is our standing in relation to the ministry? I believe that with this point there is much confusion. You hear many saints using this phrase, "the ministry". But I would say they are misusing it, and abusing it. They are not using it at all properly. This kind of speaking, "We are for the ministry,", or, "They are not for the ministry" has been heard by most all of us.

First, I want to define what the ministry is according to the truth. Very briefly, according to God's Word, the unique ministry is the dispensing of God into His people to produce the Church. This is a simple statement of the truth. Now, let me ask you, Are you for the ministry? This is the ministry. However, in most cases, I think that when we use this term, we just mean a certain person's ministry. No, saints, we all should be ministers in this one unique ministry. It is not the exclusive ministry of any one person. We must realize this. Acts 1:17 speaks of Judas having lost the ministry. It says that he "had his portion in this ministry." All the twelve had their portion. And, we all have our portion in this ministry.

You may say, "Well aren't there some especially gifted ones who are in this ministry?" Yes, there are the apostles, prophets, evangelists, shepherds and teachers. But, they are all plural. This is a corporate matter. There are many in this ministry. And we all have a share, a portion in this one unique ministry of God being dispensed into His people to build up the Body of Christ. Hallelujah! I hope that we could have a new kind of speaking, that when we talk about the ministry, we will all be clear that we are not talking about any one person's ministry. If you are talking about one person's ministry, then say so. If it's Brother so-and-so's ministry, say "Brother so-and-so's ministry." May we all have a renewed understanding regarding the meaning of the ministry and our part in it.

8. I now come to the eighth point: what is our standing in relation to the apostles? According to God's Word, apostles are always plural. Recently I looked up this word in the concordance. It is used only in the singular when it refers to a specific person, like "Paul, an apostle of Jesus Christ;" or, "Peter, an apostle of Jesus Christ." All the other times, it is plural: e.g., "He gave some apostles…" (Eph. 4). There were the twelve apostles, and many other apostles. You have the apostles' fellowship, which is s', not 's. They continued steadfastly in the apostles' (plural) fellowship, and in the apostles' (plural) teaching. I think we all need some calibration in this point also. The apostles are plural. But, I'm afraid that if you asked most saints in the churches today, "How many apostles are there?" They would say, "One,…only one." No, brothers and sisters, there are many apostles today. Some of you may wonder, "Who are they?" Well, I could tell you a number of them. Anyway, the apostles are plural, according to God's Word.

Furthermore, the many apostles, with all the gifted members, are given for the building up of the Body of Christ, not for building up their own work, their ministry. They are for the Body. So what should our attitude be toward these apostles? We should receive from them anything of life and truth, anything they may have which will help us and benefit us for the building up of the Body. We all should be willing to receive from all the apostles. The New Testament gives us many examples of a number of apostles being in very good fellowship and coordination. First Corinthians shows that Paul and Apollos were in good relationship of mutual respect and coordination. Paul commended Apollos, calling himself a planter, and Apollos a waterer (I Cor. 3). In chapter 16, he recommends and urged Apollos to go to visit Corinth. Also, in Titus 3:13, Paul says, When Zenas and Apollos come to you, send them on their way; take care of them. The apostles had a mutual love and care for one another, and a good coordination together. Saints, we all surely need one another. And apostles need one another. No one man is complete or all-inclusive.

We must see another point about the apostles, which Paul emphasized in I Corinthians 4:6, "Now these things brothers, I have applied to myself and Apollos for your sakes, that you may learn in us not to go beyond what has been written." In other words, do not exalt us, or consider us, beyond what has been written. And, what has been written? Chapter 4 refers back to chapters 1-3. In chapter 3, Paul said, "I planted, and Apollos watered, but GOD made to grow. So that, neither is the one who planted anything, nor the one who watered, but the One who made to grow, GOD." Do not go beyond that! Then in 4:1, he continues, "in this way, let a man so account of us as servants of Christ, and stewards of the mysteries of God."

Don't you remember what was happening in Corinth? They were exalting this one and that one. Some were saying that they were of Paul, others of Cephas, and others of Apollos. They were exalting certain ones beyond what had been written. Saints, we should not exalt any apostle or any servant of the Lord beyond what is written. If we do, we fall into the very situation of Corinth, and the result will be the same, division! I hope we would not do this. Again, I must say that we are not against anyone. We should love, honor and respect everyone, especially the apostles and ministers which the Lord has given to His Body. But we should never go beyond what is written.

May we all take the proper standing based upon these eight points. This will save us from many troubles, and we will be enabled to go in a proper good way.

Brother Godfred Otuteye: The points which John has just shared are very important for us to understand the practical things I am going to share. For the church to go on we must understand the importance of the genuine oneness of the Body. You see, some of the items I will mention tonight have already been used by some as the ground of oneness: e.g., if a certain person does not practice certain things, he is condemned as not being "one with the ministry." But these things I will mention are not items of the ground of the oneness of the church. This is why it is critical that we all be clear concerning them.

9. First is the church administration. We all sang that line in Hymn 824, Administration local, each answering to the Lord. We have sung this many times, and we know it, but we do not practice the reality! This has resulted in a lot of trouble among us. The spiritual oversight and practical administration of things in a local church are the responsibility of the elders thee. They must bear the responsibility for the shepherding, teaching, and practical care of the church in their locality. The elders do not become a class of people who replace the brothers and sisters. No, they and the saints should do the Lord's work there, with the elders having the oversight over this work under the direct Headship of Christ Himself.

The local church does not have any headquarters, but only the Headship of the Lord Himself. In the early days we often heard it said: We have no headquarters; neither do we have any head office. The local churches should not be subject to any central control. Saints, the church in Anaheim should not be subject to any headquarters, head office, or central control, except that which comes down from the third heavens! However, this does not mean that we do not fellowship with the apostles who have founded the churches. We do have mutual fellowship with others. But in the administration of any fellowship, in the carrying out of that fellowship, if the elders should decide to carry it out, it is their responsibility. Please note how in I Corinthians 5, even though Paul told the church in Corinth that they had to excommunicate that sinful brother, Paul did not excommunicate him. The church there did it. Paul gave them the teaching, what was right according to God's principle; but its out-working was the responsibility of the elders there with the church.

Why am I saying so much about this point? Because in the last few years we have not practiced this in Anaheim. I would even say this – and because I am one of the brothers taking the lead here, the Lord cover me – I would say that to a certain extent we brothers abdicated our responsibility to the Lord and to the church here. We came under the influence and pressures of a lot of external things. Many activities of the Lord's work became the source, directing our church. There was a period of time here when we were changing course every few weeks.

First, we closed the meeting hall down and sent everybody home; then we called everybody back! However, I am not criticizing anyone else for doing this. The criticism should mostly be upon us, because we had the responsibility to see what was right and best for the church here; and we were not faithful to the Lord in this matter.

Tonight, I am representing the other brothers here to apologize to the church. During these past months, when we began to see what has been happening to us, we have very much repented to the Lord. But we owe all of you an apology. We feel that what we did was wrong, and we should not practice this anymore. Whatever comes out of the Lord's speaking anywhere, the brothers taking the responsibility in a particular church ought to pray and seek the Lord to see if that is the right thing for their locality at that time. There are many wonderful things in the Scriptures, and many wonderful things which the Lord's servants are speaking; but we do not practice everything at the same time. Some things are good for this moment, while some will be good for tomorrow; and some things may not be right for us to do at all. It is the responsibility of the leading brothers along with the whole church to seek the Lord and His guidance as to what is right for us in our locality at any particular time. In the past, certain ones have come to the elders, speaking very strongly, "How come we are not practicing such and such, because this was spoken last night at such and such a place? If our church is going to be one with the ministry, we have to do this right away!" Well, saints, we would like to make it very clear, that our not practicing what was spoken last night does not mean that we do not accept it or receive it. However, it may not be the right thing for us at this time. Too much in the past we have zig-zagged this way and that! We have wasted and lost a lot of time. Many saints became confused and lost heart, not coming to the meetings anymore. Some even feel that the elders do not know what they are doing. And it does look that way.

10. The second thing I need to share is concerning the Living Stream Ministry Office. In the last few years this office and its management has been promoted exceedingly among us, and even exalted among us. This statement was made: "To be one with the Living Stream Ministry Office and its management is to be one with the apostle." (This is an exact quote). And, conversely, not to be one with the Living Stream Ministry Office is to not be one with the apostle. Furthermore, in the environment of this kind of pressure and promotion, we elders in Anaheim joined together with many other brothers to declare publicly our oneness with this. I believe that when we did this we were representing you, declaring that the church here was one with the Living Stream Ministry Office and its management. These very things were spoken in some of our meetings.

We feel that we must address these issues tonight because we did something publicly, and it was wrong; therefore, we should take care of it publicly. We declared our oneness with the Living Stream Ministry Office and its management. Then, due to such promotion, that office began to exercise a level of influence over some of the churches – I dare not say all of them, but certainly including Anaheim – and over the young people's work, to a degree that we today consider objectionable. We do not agree with this, and we also will not stand for this. Since we declared publicly that we were one with this office, even so, we now must make it clear that it is inappropriate for the church as an organic, divine entity to be one with a business office. These two things are not compatible!

Furthermore, there have been certain practices and conduct in the Living Stream Ministry Office which we find intolerable. We want to say here openly that as the church in this locality, we disassociate ourselves from those practices and that conduct. Again, the reason we are doing this is because you saints were put under the impression that because we publicly declared our oneness with this office, therefore we are one with everything going on there. This is why we must publicly undo what we have done. Again, I must confess that the blame for our church's improper relationship with the Living Stream Ministry Office must be borne by us elders; it should not be put on the doorstep of that office. For a period of time, we – and I took considerable lead in this matter, but all the brothers feel responsible for this, and acknowledge having done it – we publicly promoted these things and this office. We pressed the saints and even pushed them to serve there, and to be one with that office and its management. Even to some extent I encouraged the saints to shut their mouths, no matter what they saw, or what happened. Forgive us for this! We want to tell the church that we are sorry.

The Living Stream Ministry Office is a business office, engaged in the publishing, distribution and sales of Christian literature. Our relationship with that office should have been at this level, and nothing more. The Living Stream Ministry Office has no authority over this church. And the church here is under no obligation to serve there. (Your decision to work there as an employee, or to serve there, is your own personal decision, not a matter of the church). We hope that this matter is very clear to all of us now, so that we may go on properly in the church here.

11. Next, I want to share regarding matters related to Life-Studies and to Christian literature in general: our reading of Christian literature other than the Bible can be a great help to our spiritual life. In I Timothy, Paul asked Timothy to bring the scrolls which he had left at Troas. He also said, "And especially the parchments..." You may say that these were all Scriptures; but we could also say that there may have been other materials which were also helpful to Paul in his work. Anyway, this does indicate that Paul had some kind of library! Be that as it may, our point is that the reading of spiritual books is edifying to us. We encourage you to read any Christian literature which you find edifying, doing so at your discretion.

However, we would like to say that none of us should ever allow these spiritual materials to become a crutch or a replacement for the reading of our Bible. It does not matter what material or whose material it is. It is too easy for these things which are a help to us to become a replacement, just as spiritual leaders can so easily become a replacement for the Lord Himself. We must never allow this to happen. Furthermore, for anyone to insist that the saints have to read only the materials published by the Living Stream Ministry is altogether too much. Anyone among us who holds this concept, or insists upon this is going too far, for it turns our church into a sect. On the other hand, to oppose the reading of footnotes, Life-Studies, or books published by the Living Stream Ministry is also sectarian. We don't agree with that either. All of you should have the full liberty to read any Christian literature which you find edifying. Then, if in a meeting a saint wants to read a certain point, a footnote, or something which has helped him, we all should be open to receive it. But we should not insist that everyone do it. We hope that you all are clear about this matter now.

12. Our next point is concerning the Book sales, which we have here in the hall. We are operating this service strictly as a non-profit service to you all. Some of you who are against this may ask me to show you a Bible verse which says we can sell something in the hall. Well, there is no Bible verse to tell us to use air-conditioning or electricity! Saints, if you press any point too far, the whole thing becomes ridiculous. In all of these practical matters, we should exercise the spirit of generality: i.e., if a thing is not sinful an it is useful to the saints, then it is okay.

We have this service as a convenience for you. After the meetings it is much easier to just go back there and buy any books which you need, rather than having to go to a bookstore. But during the past few years, especially since I have been here, we have done far too much advertising and merchandising of certain books. And in our spirit, when we considered this whole matter before the Lord, we realized it has been altogether too much. The church meeting should not be turned into the merchandising of any materials. Things have their place, and it is not appropriate to do this here. So, we will continue this service, but we will no longer advertise or promote any books. All of you are free to go afterward to see what is new, what is old, or what is what. Also, you who do not agree with us having a book sales service, you are free not to us it; you may go to any bookstore outside to buy. But as a convenience for you who want to get materials here, whether they are published by the Living Stream Ministry or by anyone else, we make this service available to you.

13. Another point we must make clear to you concerns the semi-annual Trainings. Many saints have attended these trainings at one time or another and have received help from them. However, we now feel that from this time onward we will no longer interrupt our church life during the trainings. If any of you wish to attend a training, feel free to do so. That is your own personal decision. And if there is a video training, we will make a room available in the hall for you who wish to attend. But for you saints who do not attend a training, our church life will continue on a regular schedule during the time the training is taking place, so you may attend the meetings here. We brothers think this is fine and good. We will not close our doors, or stop any meetings, or do anything which will disturb our schedule. If we are in Ephesians during the training, we will continue in it. But I say again, if you want to go, just go; if you don't want to go, don't go; and you may attend the regular meetings of the church here if you wish.

14. Another point we must cover is, what is our standing in relation to the other churches? We should respect and highly esteem all other churches, whether they are small or large. And we should have full fellowship with all of them with a good traffic between us and them. After all, we are members one of another, we are all of the one Body of Christ. However, we here do not want the elders of any other church to be telling us what to do. I feel very sorry that we have let this kind of thing happen here in Anaheim.

When I was in Irvine, I remember telling some brothers: "Never come back from visiting another church and put our church down because of what you have seen there." This kind of thing used to happen a lot. If we see something good in another church, we might minister that to the saints, but we should not compel the church in our place to begin right away to practice like some other church. No, we should seek the Lord about this matter: what does He want for us in our locality?

15. Another point we must clarify is regarding practices: e.g., to practice things like door-knocking. I am mentioning this matter because this happened recently: last year our church almost had a division over this! So we must state that in all these matters we must practice generality with all the saints. Any practice which is not sinful, we should not oppose; but, neither should we impose it. There should be no persuasion and no

opposition, no insisting and no resisting, in any practice. I can testify that shortly after I was saved, I did a lot of door-to-door preaching of the gospel, and a lot of people got saved. There is nothing wring with preaching the gospel in this way. However, when we brothers said that everybody had to practice this way, this was altogether too much and was against the principle of generality. Tonight, we would like the church here to be clear that we stand against this kind of thing. We should not force anyone to do anything in practice.

I also remember clearly how last year, for many meetings, those who were going out door-knocking literally took over the church meetings. They gave testimonies about this and about that; but the rest of the church became totally disgusted with this. Saints, these kind of things should not have happened to us. We are surely open to receive from those who practice a certain thing, but it should not be forced upon anyone. We must be very general regarding any practice.

16. My final point is concerning this matter of the Gospel. We brothers really hope and pray that out of your enjoyment of the Lord, you all will preach the gospel to your neighbors, to your friends and to people around you, preaching it widely, and preaching it daily! However, we must make it clear that there is no one particular way in which we must preach the gospel. Any proper way is good. (We should not appreciate using rock-n-roll or movies, or any worldly means to attract people to the Lord; but, any proper way of preaching is okay.) If you invite people to your home, that is good, and to go to their home is good. But none of us should insist upon any particular way of gospel work, or it will again cause division in the church. No, the church is one Body it is organic and living!

These are the practical points we brothers wish to share with you. Again, we are sorry for the things which we have done wrong, and we ask the Lord and you all to forgive us. Furthermore, our reason for having this fellowship is not to vindicate anyone or to condemn anyone, or to do anything for ourselves. We are having this fellowship for the purpose of bringing us all back to the Lord Himself. He is our Head, He is our center; and He should be the entire, unique content of the church life! We hope that the things we have briefly mentioned will clear up the past so that we all can go forward together positively as the church in our city.

Brother Albert Knoch: It is so good to hear tonight's fellowship, and I just want to confirm by a testimony the clear standing which the brothers have presented. I recently visited some churches in Europe. They didn't know about all the turmoil we have been in, but I believe that all of them would agree with our standing here tonight. There is nothing wrong with what has been shared; the Word of God teaches these truths. Of course, we are not here to oppose anything which the Lord has given us through the years. But I must say that as I listened to the fellowship in the localities in Europe, I heard just about the same things. They are asking: "Are we really the local church with a general standing, open to every Christian in our city? Or, are we a sect?" They, like us, are concerned, because through their practices over the past few years – and they were trying to follow what they considered the up-to-date, present move of the Lord – they found out that gradually they were becoming a very special kind of "church", not a local church (i.e., in their meetings they read only certain materials, etc.) I don't know exactly how the Lord will bring us out of this condition we have gotten into, but I do feel that what the brothers have shared about the proper standing and practices will help a lot. When I was in Europe, in a church meeting there, even though I could not understand their language, I realized in my spirit that anything which is not Christ is just not the church! The church is just Christ. Oh, saints, any fearfulness on our part has to be taken away; we must not be afraid of just following Christ, and of having Him alone as our unique Head! I saw some saints who were not "following the ministry" the way we thought we had to. I saw these saints enjoying the Lord so much, loving Him and serving Him, and being more fruitful than myself, even leading many to the Lord and bringing them into the church life. They are open to Brother Lee's ministry, as well as to ministry from many others. They just enjoy them all and use whatever they can. When a certain practice comes, they just look to the anointing within them; and, if they feel led to do it, they just do it. If they don't feel led to, they just don't do it. They are under no obligation to please anyone but the Lord Himself. They all come together to enjoy Christ and share Him for the building up.

I feel I also have to apologize to you for my part in all the promotions and the things which I have done and said. Our heart has always been to do what is good for the building up of the church. But we have realized that we must not bring in anything except Christ. I do appreciate this word about the New Testament ministry being all our responsibility: even if you are with just one other brother, and you are in your spirit ministering Christ, you are ministering the New Testament ministry to him! You are building up the church at that time, and you are being perfected in the ministry.

Oh, saints, the Lord has put us all on the ground of the oneness of His Body in this locality, and we just have no way to leave. We have to stay here until we are keeping the oneness of the Spirit and arriving at the oneness of the faith, until we grow up into the full reality of the One who said that He would build His church. I am very aware that the one whom the Lord Jesus called a stone, was just a few minutes later called by Him, Satan! Thus whenever we get into our natural man, we are capable of all kinds of mistakes and of doing much damage. Nevertheless, we must still stay together on the ground of oneness in our locality until all these things are dealt with, and we have the pure church (the Bride), which is just the Lord Himself built up in us, through us, and with us!

APPENDIX C

AN OPEN LETTER TO THE SAINTS IN ANAHEIM

Jan. 7, 1989

Dear Brothers and Sisters,

A number of issues and questions have been raised recently in the church in Anaheim which require our response. We felt that we, john Ingalls and Albert Knoch, should make our standing known in writing for the benefit of all the saints. There are six main points which are addressed in these pages, the last of which, entitled, "How do we go on?" especially needs our attention and consideration I these days.

We are also attaching to this letter a corrected and edited copy of the transcript of a meting held in Anaheim, August 28, 1988, in which are 16 points presenting the standing of the church.

The six matters raised with our response are as follows:

1. Transcripts of the meeting held in Anaheim on August 28, 1988

a. Should their distribution be denounced?

b. Who do these statements represent

It is true that we did not authorize the printing and distribution of the transcripts of that meeting, nor did we know that it was being done until after they were already in circulation. At that time, we attempted to restrain the distribution, but to no avail. Later, after further consideration, we felt that the distribution of the transcripts covering the sixteen points spoken by John Ingalls and Godfred Otuteye plus the confirming testimony given by Albert Knoch, was allowed sovereignly by the Lord and used by Him. We deeply feel that these points are solidly based on the Word of God and need to be reviewed, addressed, and considered by all the saints. Of course, some of the points spoken by Godfred were especially suited to the local situation in Anaheim and should be viewed as such; this should be clear to all who read it.

In the light of the above, we do not feel that we can or should denounce the distribution of this document either in Anaheim or by letter to other churches. If any church communicates with us concerning this matter, we will share our attitude and convictions with them (as we have already done in some instances). We are attaching a corrected and edited copy of the transcript to this letter.

Concerning the separate distribution of testimonies given by others in the meeting of August 28th, we had no involvement in that, and though not agreeing with it, do not feel obliged to denounce it.

It is clear from the transcript that we did not purport to represent all the saints or all elders. We spoke for ourselves as elders, expressing what we felt the standing of the church should be based on the Word of God. We felt then and still feel strongly that these points are well supported by the truth. They have been confirmed by many saints and elders, both here and in other localities, and many feel they have been greatly helped by them. Actually, they are for the greater part what we have always believed and taught I the Lord's recovery since the beginning. Should any of the saints have any difficulties with these points, we encourage them to indicate these specifically in writing, based on the Word, and send them to us. We would be happy to address the matters in further fellowship.

2. Distribution of the flyer entitled Significant Dates in the History of the Church in Anaheim.

Except for a few minor inaccuracies which do not affect the substance of the flyer, the contents are factual. Despite this, we cannot agree with its tone. We feel it is wholly out-of-character and unbecoming to Christians to distribute such a flyer anywhere. We as elders, certainly hope it will not be distributed on the premises of our meeting hall or in any place where the saints are gathered.

3. Dealing with various disturbing testimonies given by saints in the meetings during September and October.

Concerning some of the statements made by the saints deemed offensive and untrue, we would remind you that Godfred already publicly denounced and rebuked these, and we concurred. We would encourage the saints who were offended and grieved by other matters shared to go directly to the brothers themselves according to the Lord's teaching in Matthew 18. We have spoken privately to a number of the saints whose speaking may have offended others, advising them to consider before the Lord what kind of action if any He would have them to take.

4. Our relationship with Brother Lee

a. Allowing the saints the freedom of close fellowship with him.

b. Concerning the announcement of meetings, trainings, and new books.

We acknowledge that "the church in Anaheim has had a long and close relationship with Brother Lee." Therefore, as you expressed in your letter, we certainly desire "to be fair to all the saints and allow the same freedom of close fellowship." Our attitude is that we would like to practice true generality, where all the saints are free to follow their own conscience (see point #6 of this letter). If any of the saints desire to receive Brother Lee's ministry by attending trainings and conferences of his or by reading his books, they are at full liberty to do so. If any prefer not to do this, we should also afford them this liberty. We do not agree, however, that Brother Lee or any other servant of the Lord should ever be made an issue or factor of division.

Concerning the announcement of meetings, conferences, and trainings; if properly informed, we will announce the meetings of Brother Lee and other servants of the Lord which we deem appropriate and helpful at the time for the Lord's purpose and economy. Concerning the announcement of new books, we will abide by our statement I the attached transcript concerning this (point #12).

5. Brother Joseph Fung's visit to Anaheim

We feel strongly that we should receive all brothers, all whom the Lord receives. Joseph himself is a servant of the Lord who has served in the church in Hong Kong for many years, and we honor him as such. Whether or not his presence here is profitable for the church, only the Lord truly knows and can judge. We surely do not have any jurisdiction to ask him to leave this area. In fact, we consider that his visit has been helpful to many of the saints. Some discouraged ones have been restored, and some angry ones have been calmed down. We feel that our fellowship with him has been constructive and useful for the building up of the church. Moreover, we consider that some things that have been spread concerning him are slanderous and evil reports.

6. How do we go on?

We believe that all the saints among us love Christ and the church. Moreover, we also feel that we need to go on positively, not only with a few saints, but with all. Therefore, we are happy to have this opportunity to share with you our burden in this regard. We believe we can answer this question under four headings:

a. By receiving the Word of God

Our greatest need is for the Lord t speak to us through His Word. Therefore we strongly encourage every saint to earnestly seek the Lord every day in His Word, not only reading it, but receiving the Lord's speaking through it. His speaking is the most crucial thing. We all need it desperately and should pray that the Lord will definitely speak to us every day through His Word. Matthew 4:4 says that man shall live by every word that proceeds out of the mouth of God. Without the Lord's speaking it is impossible to go on or have a proper church life. Only this will deliver us from many distracting considerations and focus us on the Lord Himself and His purpose. Only this will richly supply us to share the living Word in the meetings to nourish others and build up the Body. The best way to overcome many troubling factors is to be well-nourished by the living, spoken Word of God.

Moreover, our church life and daily life should be governed in all things solely by the Word of God, not by any expediency, tradition, or extraneous influence. (See point #1 of the attached transcript.) May the Lord fully establish the authority and supremacy of His Word among us.

b. By following the Spirit's leading

In order to do this, we must give the Lord His rightful place as our unique Head, the Head of the church (Col. 1:18) and the Head of every man (I Cor. 11:3). This means that as the church in Anaheim we are directly responsible and accountable to the Lord (Rev. 2 & 3), and need to receive our leading in all things from Him. This also means that as individual members of His Body we are directly responsible and accountable to Him who is now the Spirit within us. Therefore, it is our privilege and responsibility to be led directly by the Spirit (Rom. 8:14) and taught by His anointing concerning all things (I Jn. 2:27). This is a great blessing of the new covenant. In this age there is no intermediary between ourselves and Him. We hope that in all areas of the church life and our daily lives we will increasingly experience this reality.

In order to seek the Lord's leading in all things we feel deeply that we need much more earnest prayer than we now have. We have had a great shortage of this I the past. May the Lord send us to our knees, especially at this time, corporately, individually, or in small groups, to seek His mercy, His grace, and His leading for our going on.

c. By practicing and keeping the oneness of the Spirit

To do this we must learn to receive all whom God receives, and to receive one another as Christ has received us to the glory of God (Rom. 15:7). We hope that in all our meetings and church life we may receive every brother and sister with the love and grace of Christ, regardless of their concepts or convictions; and when they participate in the meetings, may we stand with them in one spirit, praying for them and opening ourselves to receive their portion. We also hope that the oneness we keep will not be less in scope than the whole Body of Christ, and that we will come out of any party or sectarian oneness that excludes other members. May the Lord grant us His abundant grace that we will not allow any issue concerning persons, practices, or teachings to divide us.

Moreover, to keep the oneness we must learn to practice the proper generality in our attitude toward one another (see point #15 of the attached transcript), allowing each one the freedom to follow his own conscience and convictions in all things, but not allowing any differences to become a dividing factor. This will surely test us, exposing our narrowness and smallness. May the Lord enlarge our hearts and fill us with His love toward all. In Anaheim at present we have the best environment to practice what we have so long taught but very little lived. What a testimony this will be! Let us seek to keep the Lord's word in Ephesians 4:2-3 regarding longsuffering and forbearance toward all when faced with provocations. And let us learn, as we have heard many times, neither to impose or oppose, but to hold the truth (Christ Himself) in love. May the Lord enlighten and strengthen us all!

d. By preaching the gospel to the unbelievers and shepherding the saints

We sincerely hope that the Lord will fully raise up among us a healthy, normal gospel preaching with His rich blessing. We feel this is vital to our going on and indispensable to the normal church life. Hence, we pray that the Lord will enable the saints to preach the gospel in their daily lives in many ways. If some saints desire to share the gospel of Christ by knocking on doors, we praise the Lord for that and encourage them to do it. But we are mainly concerned that the brothers and sisters would have a daily life of gospel preaching and fruit-bearing with all their friends, neighbors, classmates, and colleagues. Most of all, we hope that we may have a happy church life as a strong base and impetus for the spread of the gospel.

With the gospel preaching we need adequate shepherding of all the new believers with the best use of home gatherings, either in their homes or the homes of the saints. Furthermore, the saints themselves surely need much mutual shepherding. We hope that all our homes would be used in this way, and that they would be filled with edifying fellowship in the Word.

May the Lord grant us all much mercy and grace that we may be preserved for His purpose and go on to satisfy Him as His testimony in this locality. May we all pray for this.

Your brothers in Christ,

John C. Ingalls

Albert P. Knoch

APPENDIX D

LETTER NOTIFYING BROTHER LEE OF OUR RESIGNATION

Dear Brother Lee,

As you know, during the last months we both have tried to stand here in Anaheim to see if some of our serious concerns regarding the church practice could be resolved. After so much time, the situation indicates that it is not profitable for either us or the saints to go on in this way. In all honesty to ourselves, to the saints, and to the Lord, and for the sake of our genuineness before all, we feel that we must at this time withdraw from the eldership. We cannot hold the position of elders and take the lead in a way that is not accepted and even opposed by some of the saints. The course which some saints insist upon taking is not one in which we can lead them.

Tomorrow morning, March 19th, at the close of the meeting, we will announce our withdrawal from the eldership to the saints with a brief word of explanation. We have full peace before the Lord and feel very clear in taking this step, although we feel grieved that the nature of the recovery has so changed and developed to the point where we are forced to do this. We believe that our concerns have already been made known to you through our meetings together last year; so we will not repeat them here. We hope to continue in fellowship with the saints as fellow-members of the Body of Christ, and wish to let you know how much we appreciate all the teachings from the Word which have helped us to know the Lord and His church. We have no bitterness whatever toward yourself, or anyone, but only wish that we could have been more useful to the Lord in the past years.

You are in our prayers, as are all the churches under your ministry. We wish you the very best in the Lord. With greetings in Him,

Your brothers in Christ,

John Ingalls

Albert Knoch

APPENDIX E

RESIGNATION STATEMENT OF JOHN INGALLS AND AL KNOCH

March 19, 1989

John Ingalls:

Last week, as Brother Al Knoch and I were praying and fellowshipping together concerning the church, we became very clear before the Lord that at this time we need to withdraw from the eldership in Anaheim. We want to make that known this morning, and we are taking that step this morning to withdraw from the responsibilities and duties of the eldership. We would like to give a little word of explanation why we feel to take this step at this time.

Firstly, I would give a little testimony from my heart to you all. It has been about 28 or 29 years now since I first saw the vision of Christ and the Church. That was indeed very precious, and I was riveted by it. What a mercy that I could see Christ, the all-inclusive Christ and the church as His Body; even more, to see the ground of oneness! That vision has held me all these years; it has preserved me and strengthened me and enabled me to go on. I have never lost that vision and still desire to be obedient to it.

But a year and a half ago this very month I began to realize that our practices have differed and deviated from our vision. Our vision was the same, our teaching was mostly the same, the truth is always the same, but our practice has really differed. Our practice has not at all matched our teaching. This has been a grief and a deep concern to me. The Lord knows how much this is so.

Not only that, but a year and a half ago I also began to realize that the nature of what we call the Lord's recovery has changed. This also was a great concern. When the nature changes, that is serious, very serious.

Yesterday and today, I wrote down a few points which I would like to mention briefly without much elaborating. These points embody my concerns and give the basis upon which we are making this decision this morning.

1. There has been a change of emphasis to the building up of the work or the ministry more than the local churches. When we first received the vision of the church we heard time and time again that the ministry is for the churches. But it seems that in the past years this has been turned around. there has been more emphasis on the churches being for the ministry. The ministry has been promoted, exalted, and built up, and the churches have suffered greatly in the process.

2. There has been a great effort and promotion to unite the saints and the churches around a certain leader and organization, and we cannot agree with that.

Some of you may be familiar wit a little book that's been printed by the Living Stream Ministry. We've had it for many years, The Beliefs and Practices of the Local Churches. I would surely agree that these are our beliefs, but I would have to say concerning some of the things, they are not our practices. I would like to read one short paragraph here. At the end of the book some questions are asked, and one of them is: "Who is our leader?" (page 16). The answer is:

"Our unique leader is Christ. We have no official, permanent, or organized human leadership. Furthermore, there is no hierarchy of any kind and no world-wide leader. We regard no person as infallible, and we do not follow anyone blindly. On the contrary, we follow only those whose teaching and practice is in accordance with the truth of God's Word...."

Now this, I believe, we would all subscribe to and say that's our belief. But I'm sorry to say, that has not been our practice.

3. There has been much pressure with full expectation that all the saints and the churches will conform to the burden of the ministry and be identical with one another in full uniformity of practice, to carry it out. This also we cannot agree with.

4. In February 1986 there was an elders' training in Anaheim, and Al and I were there. During that time, a strong word was released concerning all the churches being identical and everyone following the ministry with its one leadership absolutely. At the end of that training, the brothers wrote a letter which, with perhaps two or three exceptions, we all signed. Brother Al Knoch and I signed that letter. There were 419 signatures of elders, so many that it required 27 pages to include them all. That letter is duplicated in the Elder's Training Vol. 8 if you desire to look at it.

At present time and for the past year and a half, we have regretted very much that we signed that letter, and even more, that such a letter was ever written. There is no precedent of that in the Word; furthermore there is no scriptural basis for the contents of such a letter. We agreed in that letter that we would be identical with all the churches, that we would follow the ministry absolutely, and that we realized Brother Lee's leading was indispensable to our oneness. Then at the bottom of the letter, we said that all these things were according to the teaching of the Word of God. But those things are not according to the teaching of the Word, and we regret very much that we subscribed to them. I want to state publicly and make it clear that I would retract my signature.

5. There has been quite an emphasis, at least in practice, on a kind of centralization of the churches and the work, which we also find contrary to the Word of God.

6. There has been a pervasive control exercised over the church. Now at least I can speak for Anaheim. I know this to be a fact, and I'm in a position to know this. There has been much outside influence exercised upon the church which has made it very difficult to go on by getting our leading directly from the Lord. This control has not been

exercised so much directly, but very much indirectly, through videos, conferences, trainings, and elders' meetings.

7. Church history reveals that in the history of one denomination after another, not all started as a denomination. There was a fresh move of the Lord. The Lord did something among His people in a fresh way, with His presence and blessing. But after the saints in that group multiplied and other groups were formed, they all agreed together and decided to affiliate in order to preserve what they had received.

The second thing they did again and again was to start a training center, a Bible School, or a Seminary to educate their people in the truth they had received. From there on out, it was a full-blown denomination. The first step is affiliation under one leadership; the second is some sort of training center. That is the way group after group has gone, and, sorry to say, we are also going that way. I have to speak honestly, and I regret it very much. I wish we could reverse that process.

8. I must say truthfully from my heart that I very much appreciate Brother Lee's portion; it has been a great portion from the Lord which has brought blessing to us all. But, honestly speaking, he has been exalted and honored above what is written, according to I Corinthians 4:6. This surely is unmistakable, and we regret this very much. We repent of having ourselves taken part in this.

One of the brothers said to me at one time, "I'm going to put a sign up outside the meeting hall here – The Local Church of Witness Lee." I would hate that there would be in reality any such thing, but here has been a strong tendency toward this. The church should not be the church of anyone but Christ.

9. Our oneness is not based on any spiritual leader, gifted person, or teaching. A spiritual leader should never be made an issue or a factor of division, but Brother Lee and his ministry have been made a great issue and factor of division among us.

10. In Matthew 22 the Lord was speaking to the Pharisees. They were asking Him all kinds of questions, trying to trick Him and catch Him. Then He asked them the question, "What do you think of Christ? Whose Son is He?" Everyone has to answer that question, What do

you think of Christ? But I'm afraid, that question has been changed among us to read this way – "What do you think of Witness Lee? What is your relationship to him? And that kind of question should never be asked. Such a question should never become an issue or factor among us, so that our going on or our relationship with the saints and with the church is made to depend on or relationship to him. But this has been the case. When this is done, the ground of oneness is replaced with something else.

11. There is no doubt that God wants a testimony on the earth of our oneness in Christ. Hence with all saints we should practice a real oneness. We believe this, but I'm sorry, we don't practice it much. We have a teaching concerning the ground of oneness, and this matter, of course, if very precious. But I'm afraid, honestly speaking, that we have applied this teaching in a divisive and sectarian way, so that we divide ourselves fro other Christians. This is due to an improper attitude and application of the truth. We should repent of this. I repent, because I have participated in this myself. I feel that in the local churches we have become very narrow and small; narrow in view, in our outlook, and in our reception of other saints. The body is so big, but we have become so narrow. This is manifested by our attitude toward other Christians.

12. Our attitude toward other Christians is one of belittling them and thinking we're superior to them. I don't know how many times we've heard this expression, "Poor Christianity!" We say that we're speaking only of the system, not of the people, but our attitude has definitely spilled over to the people. What we need is the reality of the oneness, not just the teaching or the slogan. We have much, not only to give, but also to learn from others.

13. "Let us go forth unto Him, outside the camp, bearing His reproach." This verse in Heb. 13:13 is very much with me and has been with me for weeks. I desire to do that. I'd like to go outside of every camp, especially the camp of myself, and not only go out, but go unto Him. I'm afraid we may go out, but not go unto Him. Then that's meaningless. The Lord is still calling His sheep out of the fold, so there could be one flock with one shepherd. May the Lord bring us to Himself, outside of every fold, every camp!

14. Our oneness should be as large as the whole Body of Christ. Any oneness that is smaller than this, we should leave, we should not keep.

15. The local administration. This means that we all go directly to Him for His leading in the church here, at the same time maintaining a proper fellowship with other saints, other churches, and the Lord's servants. Regarding this, I will read a couple of sentences in this book, The Beliefs and Practices of the Local Church. The question is "Where is your headquarters?" The answer is:

"Each local church is autonomous." (page 16)

Now I have never used this word autonomy, but this word, "autonomous" is used in this book published by the Living Stream Ministry (1978):

"Each local church is autonomous in its administration, Therefore, there is no central headquarters."

And another sentence (page 19):

"In this matter, as in all administrative affairs, the local churches are autonomous and locally governed."

16. There has been to some extent an atmosphere of fear brought in among the saints and among the churches, bringing the conscience of the saints into bondage. I believe this has been done by an over-stressing and distortion of the teaching concerning deputy authority. This has brought the saints into a condition where they are fearful to follow their conscience, to be one with their spirit, and sometimes to speak their genuine concerns.

17. There has been too much emphasizing of methods more than the inner anointing, and external big success more than the experience of the inner life. This is surely a deviation from the central lane of God's economy.

18. The so-called new way is not our problem. The matters of preaching the Gospel, having home meetings, practicing mutuality in our meetings with everyone sharing are scriptural. We have no problem with these things, and we like to practice them. Indeed we have practiced them.

Actually, these things are not new. Of course, our practicing of them might be new.

So, saints, in all honesty to you all, in all honesty to the Lord, and in all honesty to ourselves, based on the above points, we feel we must withdraw from the eldership. We are not able to lead you in this way, nor are we able to lead you out of this way. Many of you feel strongly that you would like to take a certain direction, and as elders we cannot lead you in that direction. We would not like to frustrate you either, but rather let you go on with the Lord in the way you feel you should.

We're really happy that all the saints are getting into the Word more and more. That's very precious, and I encourage you all to go on in that way as much as possible. I want to say that we really love you in the Lord. The Lord knows that. We care for you, and we wish you all the very best in the Lord. You are in our prayers. You will always be in our prayers. We ask you to pray for us too. Pray for Brother All and me. If we've offended any of you saints, we ask you to please forgive us. We surely never intended to offend anyone of you. We still like to keep our fellowship with you all as fellow-members of the Body of Christ.

I'm very thankful now. I have peace with myself. I have peace with the Lord, and I have peace with all of you.

***

Al Knoch·

I am so thankful that John could share those points because I could not do it so clearly. I hold the same concerns and we have been in fellowship a lot over the last year. Before Godfred withdrew, we were in fellowship with him and also these were the same concerns we presented to Brother Lee in all our times with him. So he knows all of these things already and he has considered them, and in San Diego, I believe, he said he had brought all these matters to the Lord and he feels there's no problem concerning them.

As elders in the recovery we do have a problem with many of our practices, and there's no way we could, with a good conscience, continue on in the position without the reality. How can we lead you? We can't lead in that way and yet the recovery is going that way.

So we brothers feel, as John said, it's good for us, it's good for you, and it's good for the Lord that we withdraw at this time. The reason we didn't withdraw sooner, though we were clear to withdraw last December, is that we felt the need to stand here for these very concerns for awhile longer to see what could be done and to see how the saints would respond to this kind of stand. But the more we have done this, the more clear we have become that there will not be any change at this time in the way the recovery is going.

We realize that and just hope that you would respect the way we feel the Lord is leading us. I've been here 25 years and I haven't had hardly any contact with Christians outside of this room. Practically all my fellowship has only been with the saints in the Lord's recovery as we knew it. In the last few weeks, I've been contacting a few other Christians and I have begun to see that the Lord is really working in a lot of places in ways I didn't realize. I also have had the realization that He has His timing and His leading in people's lives and He puts them in situations and puts them through certain experiences that cause them to do certain things that others can't understand. I believe our withdrawal from the eldership might be one of those things. Some of you may not understand how we could be in this position this morning, knowing us all these years. I would beg you to trust the Lord, seeing that we're not doing this lightly. We feel compelled to withdraw not just outwardly, but inwardly. Also circumstantially the Lord has pushed us into this position.

We have received a number of letters from other elders condemning the fact that we didn't publicly rebuke those who sent out tapes of our former meetings. We hope to answer those letters soon and to apologize for anything wrong, but we felt at the time led by the Lord not to control those saints or to publicly expose them or rebuke them. We let them do what they felt they should do. In many cases, we still don't even know who they are. We didn't investigate to find out. That was their business. They felt to do it. They are responsible before the

Lord for what they have done. Now we feel we must withdraw from the eldership and we are responsible before the Lord for this action.

I want to say before I withdraw that I want to thank you all. I can never express to you how much I appreciate all the support you've given to my family over the years. If I have any regret, I regret that my service as an elder has been inadequate. I have often felt I never should have been an elder. I was not constituted for that. I was appointed so I tried my best and did whatever I was told.

But inwardly and in reality, as all the years have proved, I have felt I should not be in this position. For months and months, I've had a problem, not only with these points but also with my inadequacy to carry out this kind of function. This is what I regret. On the other hand, I am a member of the Body of Christ and I should be functioning as that member and not be put into another function. I am so relieved this morning to withdraw from something I really am not. I like to be a simple brother and a very small member of His Body.

I also want you to know that I do not regret the last 25 years. I do not regret my experiences in the local church. The Lord brought me here. You may have heard my testimony concerning how the inward spirit led me to the church in Los Angeles. When I walked into my first meeting, He said "You're home." The Holy Spirit was poured upon me the same night that I attended my first meeting. So both inwardly and outwardly, against all my doctrinal beliefs, the Lord confirmed that this is where He wanted me. I've been here 25 years and I've never doubted that the Lord brought me here. Now the Lord is leading me on, not by saying, I'm home, and not by pouring out His Spirit, but as I told you, a kind of compelling.

One thing I have prayed is that you dear saints who have known us all these years will not be afraid to have further fellowship with us. I can say before the Lord with a clear conscience that I am not a negative person. I don't want to damage Brother Lee or the recovery, rather I pray for them both every day. So I beg you not to be afraid to have fellowship in the future. I'm not leaving the church. I can't do that unless I can unregenerate myself. I may not come to every meeting. That, I leave up to the Lord's leading. But when the Lord leads me, I want to come and when I come, I don't want to feel that I am an outcast. Otherwise, you can forget about calling yourselves a local church and just call yourselves a sect.

If I am really negative and you find through our fellowship that I am poisonous, tell me that and don't fellowship anymore. But I have no intention to say anything negative; rather, I just want to speak about Christ. Our desire now is to follow Him. And we cannot follow Him with a clear conscience without withdrawing from the eldership. So as long as this is clear, I don't need to say anymore. I believe that all of you have the same desire to follow Him. So if you respect His leading for me and I respect His leading for you, I believe we will all end up in the same place: the Body of Christ.

So I'm very happy. I am quite relieved to have this matter over with and I feel comforted that you have been so receptive to our withdrawal. I believe others are prepared to lead you on. I think there will be no problem. Let us pray for one another and gather together as much as we can as the Lord leads us. Let us pray that the Lord will get His testimony in the next few years before the end comes. Pray especially that the intimate love for Christ and knowledge of Christ will increase in each of us. We realize that the corporate aspect can only come out of the individual aspect. You can never be something corporately you are not individually. Let us pray that all of us may know the Lord and love the Lord much more and follow Him in such a clear way with a good conscience.

APPENDIX F

A LETTER TO THE CHURCH IN ANAHEIM FROM WITNESS LEE

March 28, 1989

The saints in Christ,
as the Church of God in Anaheim,
California, U.S.A.

Dear brothers and sisters in Christ

Greetings to all of you in the Lord.

Brothers John Ingalls and Al Knoch have written me on March 18, 1989 that they would resign from the eldership in the Church in Anaheim the very next day. And I have been informed by Brothers Philip Lin and Minoru Chen that Brothers John and Al did carry out their resignation in your morning meeting of that Lord's day. I am very sorry for the two brothers that their course in following the Lord would have had such an issue.

Now I am very much concerned for the eldership in the Church in Anaheim. After much consideration with the Lord, I feel led of the Lord to ask both Brother Eugene Gruhler in Denver and Brother Francis Ball in San Gabriel City to reassume their eldership in Anaheim in meeting the urgent need there today as they did in the past. I have fellowshipped with them about this matter and they are willing to do so. Both of them will come to Anaheim to meet you all in your morning meeting on the coming Lord's day of April 2nd. And because of my unavoidable absence from you, I would ask Brothers Philip Lin and Minoru Chen to read this letter of mine to you as my recommendation of these two brothers, Eugene Gruhler and Francis Ball, as elders to serve you all in Anaheim form this day. I do hope that this arrangement will be pleasant to all of you as it is to the Lord.

May the Lord bless you all and remember His recovery in these evil days.

A slave of Christ and your brother
in His house for His recovery,

Witness Lee

APPENDIX G

AN OPEN LETTER FROM JOHN SMITH

April 18, 1989

Dear Brothers and Sisters in San Diego,

It is now more than 17 years since I came to San Diego for the church life. There have been days of happiness and days of sadness, days nearly free of problems and days of struggle. I remember with special joy 1971-1976. Literally hundreds (especially from the Navy) were saved. We had a marvelous family church life and spontaneous blessing. I could never forget those wonderful love feasts with many saved and baptized. The quality and the degree of the blessing of those years have never returned; except perhaps during the 18 months we spent on the offerings. No doubt those 18 months were so blessed because saints were developing an exciting personal relationship to the Lord with extra-local direction held to a minimum. Some extra-local people did criticize us for continuing 18 months along that line instead of jumping to do the latest thing that came from brother Witness Lee's ministry. I never told you, but much of what I shared in those days did not come from brother Witness Lee. And I only tell you now because there is a false belief that there are little riches elsewhere. I had enjoyed many writings before I met brother Witness Lee. I gave up these writings through the years more than I should have, but the profit and joy I them was so great that I never stayed exclusively with Living Stream publications.

I appreciate the love and care I received from you all during the 17 years. Some among the Chinese-speaking saints extended themselves to the uttermost to take care of me during my long illness. Others also helped much; the other leading ones did their best to keep me from stressful situations; and all of you prayed very much. For this I am grateful. I have written this letter out of love for you all and responsibility to you.

Up to this point I have fellowshipped my standing in the present situation mainly with those who have come to see me. Recently I have realized the need to make a statement to all of you. Some have been asking, "Why doesn't John tell us where he stands?" At the judgment seat of Christ I do not want to be responsible for not telling you the truth.

I wish to say that this letter is not subtle. I am stating my realization concerning the situation among those who follow Witness Lee. I am not suggesting that brothers who differ from me are violating their conscience. That is for them to settle with the Lord just as it is for all of us. This letter will not attempt an exhaustive treatment of the matters concerned. However, as my health is considerably improved I open the door for you to come and fellowship with me if you desire.

According to my spirit, my conscience, my understanding of the Word, and the present practices, I can no longer follow brother Witness Lee. If you choose to do so that is up to you. I will love you just the same. I have no personal problems with anyone. Everyone should know the facts and be "fully convinced in his own mind" (Rom. 14:5). It is a dangerous thing for one to play the conscience for another. We are not dealing with problems of a single locality, but with serious matters of truth and practice. I believe the deviation has brought the churches following brother Witness Lee into denominationalism and sectarianism.

The points I present will be very similar to what other brothers (such as Albert Zehr, John Ingalls, etc.) have said. I have a deep realization that our practices are not according to the truth and the vision that captured me years ago: a vision of dynamic, organic, living church life unhindered by the matters explained in the following points.

1. Deputy authority and the oracle of God

I would like to preface this point by saying that the teaching concerning deputy authority is based principally on example (as opposed to the direct command of God); much from the Old Testament. It is true that "these things happened as examples for us....upon whom the end of the age has come" (1 Cor. 10:6,11). However, in scriptural interpretation one can easily go off track if he makes biblical examples equal to the commands of God. It is obvious from brother Witness Lee's sharing that he feels that he is the primary deputy authority on the earth. In the recent Pasadena conference he said "who (meaning whoever) has the deputy authority has the oracle of God." We begin with this matter because it pervades the whole conduct and atmosphere in the churches that follow Witness Lee.

Spiritual authority is endowed upon a person by the Lord. It is perceived and realized in the saints and substantiated by the Lord. As stated by Watchman Nee "we should never say so much as one word on behalf of our own authority. Rather, let us give people the liberty. The more God entrusts to us the more liberty we grant people" (Spiritual Authority pg. 121). It seems in these days there is virtually a campaign by brother Witness Lee and some others to establish his deputy authority.

Our practice has been that in nearly every conference or training we observe a declaration of authority. Old Testament cases of disobedience are cited. Often the case of Miriam's leprosy has been mentioned. But why is it not mentioned that Uzziah, Eli, and others lost their deputy authority. Furthermore, David was rebuked and chastened for the misuse of his deputy authority. No doubt Aaron lost his entrance into Canaan by being one with the disobedience of Moses when Moses struck the rock. In much of the Old Testament deputy authority was divided between priests, kings, and prophets.

In the first place deputy authorities in the Old Testament are types of Christ. Now Christ has come and Christ is the head of every man (1 Cor. 11:3). Other than Christ Himself in the Gospels the New Testament does not indicate that there will always be one chief deputy authority on the earth. Peter, Paul, and John are very prominent in the New Testament record. But we must not forget that no one today is writing Scriptures as they did. It is also plain that Paul acknowledge other groups of apostles laboring where he did not and respected their spheres of labor, although the spheres were not fully exclusive (2 Cor. 10:15 and Rom. 15:20). To say that, because in the New Testament record Peter was prominent, then Paul, and finally John, means that at all times there will be one chief deputy authority on the earth is an excessive extrapolation of New Testament examples. If brother Witness Lee considers himself to be the successor to Watchman Nee, then there must be another successor and, in principle, you have an apostolic succession similar to Roman Catholicism.

Regarding the matter of the oracles of God, Watchman Nee states, (A Table in the Wilderness For February 15) "It is our privilege to preach the Word, but no single one of us is God's oracle. We cannot utter his words without bringing to them something personal of our own. Many of us can preach a good message, but one spontaneous sentence of our has the power to confirm or overthrow it all." I would call your attention especially to 1 Pet. 4:11 which says "If any man speaks let him speak as the oracles of God" (KJV). Whether you take this as Christian teachers or anyone in an assembly, it is a plurality of believers. I will not use the space to develop this matter further in this letter.

The manner in which deputy authority has been applied, including the external standards to which all are expected to conform, has brought legality and fear into the churches. The liberty of the Holy Spirit and the freedom of the human will have been undermined. Many saints have become afraid to follow their own conscience and spirit. Also many saints have become condemned, defeated, and depressed.

2. The teaching and attempted practice of "deputy authority" and "the oracle of God", have issued in a system of control and organization of the churches. Much of the control is indirect, but nonetheless very strong. Control and organization are publicly denied but constant pressure is applied through elders' trainings, videos, conferences, and publications to push churches and brothers and sisters to conform. Surely this is strong organization.

Whatever the intention, the result of this surely hinders the organic relationship of the saint to his Lord. We have seen a great change of emphasis from "the ministry for the churches" to "the churches for the ministry." Thus the "work" or "ministry" is built up more than the local churches. Any church that would build up and exalt "the ministry" has been virtually incorporated into "the work." Since control is denied, why is honest fellowship not received? I have personally had the experience of honest fellowship not being received.

3. In recent years efforts to unite saints and churches all over the earth around a physical leader and organization have become increasingly apparent. I believe this is not scriptural. Plurality of apostles and different companies of apostles working in various areas is no longer our concept or practice. The New Testament does not present one apostle governing all the rest. Here I wish to present some notes from the Taipei Elders Training June 1989:

a. p.2 "…Don't teach differently from the minister, from Paul." But the passage in 1 Timothy does not say do not teach differently from Paul but don't teach differently from God's dispensation (or stewardship or administration), which is in faith (1 Tim. 1:4).

b. p.4 "So our burden is to pick up Brother Lee's teaching and way to make us all Witness Lees, like a Witness Lee duplication center." This should be said of no one but Christ Himself.

c. p.6 "Without this fellowship no church can be produced, built, or completed." The context of the Taipei notes implies that today this is Witness Lee's fellowship. I fully disagree with this.

d. p.13 "It may be that the number one sin in the Lord's recovery today is the improper relationship with the ministry office. It is a sign of blindness. The practical carrying out of this ministry is practically with Philip Lee." "…We love brother Lee's ministry but he has a way to do things; he does things thru the ministry office; he doesn't trust anyone else on the whole earth, so brother Lee put him (Philip) there" (p.14). Such a thing has no valid precedent in the New Testament, either by example or teaching.

The above statements from the Taipei Elders' training and more that could be presented are shocking and not according to the New Testament. The exaltation of man and chin-of-command stand out.

Since authority is ascribed and practiced in a very inorganic, organized manner, it becomes no longer spiritual authority.

4. In centralizing the work and having training centers we are going the way denominations have historically gone.

5. There has been much pressure that all the saints in the churches would conform to the burden of brother Witness Lee's ministry and carry it out in full uniformity of practice. Actually the local administration together with all the saints should go directly to the Lord for His leading in the church where they are. A proper fellowship with other saints, churches and servants of the Lord should be maintained without infringing on the proper independence of the local church. The following quotes from pages 16 to 19 of The Beliefs and Practices of the Local Churches, published in 1978 by the Living Stream ministry, are surely little practiced by the churches following brother Witness Lee. Page 16 states, "Our unique leader is Christ. We have no official, permanent, organized human leadership. Furthermore, there is no hierarchy of any kind and no world-wide leader. We regard no person as infallible, and we do not follow anyone blindly." (But blind following has been promoted among us.) "Each local church is autonomous in its administration." Page 19 states, "...in all administrative affairs the local churches are autonomous and locally governed."

6. One church one city implies that we are open to receive and accept all genuine believers. We should not demand certain practices of those with different feelings. Our attitude has been that those who have reservations concerning our practice are "unclear" and basically remain "outsiders." Those with different views are regarded as "pouring cold water", "blowing cold winds", "negative", "old", etc. These labels have characteristically been given no mater how honest a person was in the feeling he expressed. I am sorry to say that in the past I have used some of these terms regarding dear brothers and I am well aware that some of them are being used of me now.

7. The biblical truth is that the saints meet in the name of the Lord with all having freedom to share as the Spirit gives them utterance. But our practice has been to measure everyone by whether they speak "the ministry." Truth lessons, life studies, and footnotes are promoted as the

most proper ways to express anything. In some instances reading with little or no comment has been promoted. Surely this is control and must offend the Headship of the One in Whose name we meet.

8. Ministry is to dispense Christ into people for the building up of the church. All who do so have a part in God's New Testament ministry. According to our practice and our vocabulary "the ministry" is Witness Lee, and not only what he says or write but the way he says it. Anything else has "another flavor." Surely this attitude and practice is exclusive and unscriptural.

9. On what is our oneness based? Our oneness is uniquely Christ. Ephesians admonishes us to keep the oneness of the Spirit. Romans 14 admonishes us to receive one another solely on the basis of Christ, not according to any uniformity of practice. However, if one does not conform in practice, it would be a rare person who could remain comfortable among us. Furthermore, to a great extent our oneness has become based on a spiritual leader and his teaching. Brother Witness Lee and his ministry have been made a great issue and factor of division among us. At this moment some brothers and sisters might be uncomfortable in fellowship with me; because my relationship with them, to a great extent, depends upon their estimate of my relationship with Witness Lee. In Chapter 4 of The Normal Christian Church Life, Watchman Nee states that this is a failure to realize the local character of the church. The genuine ground of oneness has been replaced with other things, such as a spiritual leader, teachings, uniformity of practice, etc. In The Normal Christian Church Life (pages 92-93) Watchman Nee says, "Whenever a special leader, or a specific doctrine, or some experience or creed or organization, becomes a center for drawing together the believers of different places, then its center is other than Christ and its sphere is other than local; and whenever the divinely-appointed sphere of locality is displaced by a sphere of human invention there the divine approval cannot rest. The believers within such a sphere may truly love the Lord, but they have another center apart from Him, and it is only natural that the second center becomes the controlling one. Christ is the common center of all the churches, but any company of believers that have a leader, an experience, a creed, or an organization as their center of fellowship, will find that that center

becomes the center, and it is the center by which they determine who belongs to them and who does not." Surely this has become our case.

10. There has been too much emphasizing of "methods" more than the inner anointing, and external "big success" more than the experience of the inner life. This deviates from the central lane of God's New Testament plan. I cannot imagine that young people taking numbers in high pressure meetings to be "full time" is the real organic production of Christian workers according to the normal life of local churches as seen in the Scriptures. I have been deeply impressed with a paragraph in chapter 2 of The Normal Christian Church Life by Watchman Nee, "How grand it would be if there were no representatives of different earthly bodies, but only representatives of the Body, the Body of Christ. If thousands of local churches, with thousands of prophets and teachers, each sent out thousands of different workers, there would be a vast outward diversity, but there could still be perfect inward unity if all were sent out under the direction of one Head and on the ground of the one Body."

11. Because it has become such an issue among us, I must briefly address the matter of Philip Lee. Due to the position of influence he together with Living Stream exercised among, and to some extent, over the churches for many years, the problem of his behavior cannot be isolated to Anaheim. Neither can the problem be diminished by saying that Living Stream is merely Witness Lee's private publishing business. Through the years Living Stream has received much money in donations and multiplied thousands of dollars of free labor. Living Stream activities and influences became an integral part of the working of all the churches. Therefore, Philip's conduct and the years of failure to deal with it are matters which concern all the churches.

At the moment, I have no intention of engaging in a running controversy. However, I am not afraid of argument. I believe I know already how the points given in this letter would be answered. No doubt I the past I have used most of those arguments myself. For years many things both in our teaching and practice have troubled me. I used to defend and teach such things even when my conscience and my sprit testified to the contrary. Eventually I was forced to admit that I could no longer defend some crucial matters of the teaching and practice among us with a good conscience and a perfect spirit. There is ample substantiation for all of the above points. I do not feel it is practical to make this letter long enough to include all references. In fact, this letter is only a small part of what could be said. Rather than write pages and pages, I have opened the door for fellowship.

I write this letter to you to be faithful to the Lord. It would have been much easier to say nothing and just disappear. This the Lord would not allow me to do. This letter cannot by any means convey the clarity and fullness of thought which I have concerning these matter in these days. It may be said that to speak the things I this letter is "negative", not building up, etc. I do not accept this kind of argument. In the present situation, as I stated in the beginning of the letter, there is need to know the truth and realize the facts concerning our present teaching and practice. To use verses such as 1 Cor. 2:2, 1 Tim. 1:4, and 2 Tim. 2:23, to condemn and inhibit fellowship concerning serious deviations in truth and practice, is misapplication of the Scriptures. Everyone needs to exercise his own conscience and his own spirit. I certainly do not want to be your conscience. This is a dangerous thing to do. If I am accused of being unethical, I would remind you that the church does not belong to John Smith, Witness Lee, or any person or group of persons. It is the church of God, Christ and the saints.

I fully realize all kinds of derogatory judgments may be applied to me as a result of this letter. I am familiar with the manner in which this has been done and the terms used through the years. But as far as I know my heart is pure in these matters. I am not seeking a following or a kingdom. I am standing for what I believe to be the truth in doctrine and practice. Many of you may feel strongly to go in a certain direction with brother Witness Lee. I can neither go that way nor lead others that way. However, all of you still remain my dear brothers and sisters in Christ. My spirit is not contentious as I write; I hope yours will not be as you receive and read this letter.

Although I am saddened by the present situation, personally I am very happy in the Lord. I rejoice in renewed experience of the Headship of Christ, of reading a variety of rich material, and in thankfulness to the Lord for His great mercy upon me. My heart exults in Him. Truly His yoke is easy and His burden is light. I thank the Lord that doors of ministry are open to me here and elsewhere which, the Lord granting me more mercy, I will enter. In whatever service the Lord guides me I desire to give Him His organic way. And for myself, I like to say as Whitfield said, "Let the name of Whitfield (John Smith) perish. Let Christ be exalted."

In Christian love and concern,

John Smith

Note: This letter is not restricted to San Diego. I hope you will all read John Ingalls' and Al Knoch's statement withdrawing as elders in Anaheim.

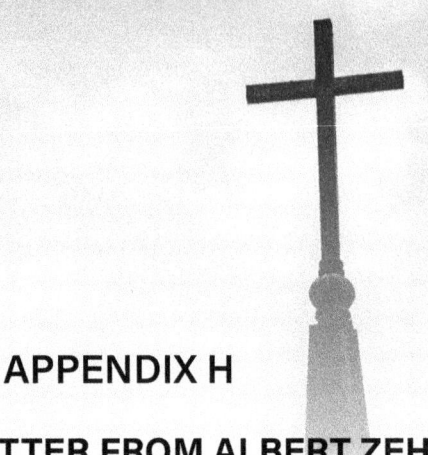

APPENDIX H

AN OPEN LETTER FROM ALBERT ZEHR

Jan. 22, 1989

Dear Brothers,

Having participated in the church-life and in elder's fellowships with some of you for over fifteen years, I trust that something has been built up between us, and that this fellowship can be received in love and sincerity. My concern for the present situation among us has become very heavy. The aspects which I list here as THE TRUTH are some of the factors which won my heart to give the past eighteen years of my life to the recovery. All of them were at some time declared and held among us. My observation is that while we may still be speaking these truths our present practice has sadly drifted. I have visited many churches in four continents during the past two years, and my decision to share these matters has come after more than one year of considering and praying about them. It seems to me that unless the Lord could have much mercy and rescue us, we have very little ground for considering ourselves other than a poor denomination.

I recognize that I owe a great debt to the recovery and have received much light and help from Bro. Lee. I feel I must however, be faithful to express what I see; in the fear of the Lord, but without fear or favor of man. Please consider these matters soberly and objectively before the Lord.

THE TRUTH vs OUR PRESENT PRACTICE

1. The WORD is our only supreme authority. All the saints should be encouraged to love it and to feel free to seek life and light from it, and to gain skill in handling and interpreting it.

OUR PRACTICE: The Word should be read in the Recovery Version and can be understood properly only with the use of the foot-notes and life-studies. No one would dare to suggest another view, nor could anyone see light beyond what has been given by "the ministry."

2. The MINISTRY is the dispensing of Christ into His saints for the building up of the church. All who minister life and the revelation of God's New Testament economy are ministers and have a part in this ministry.

OUR PRACTICE: In our present vocabulary and practice the "ministry" is Witness Lee and whatever he has written or says, and the way he says it. Anything written or spoken by another person, especially if he is not in the "recovery" is "old" or taking us backward.

3. SPIRITUAL AUTHORITY is endowed upon a person by the Lord. It will be perceived and realized in the saints and substantiated by the Lord. "We should never say so much as one word on behalf of our own authority; rather let us give people the liberty. The more God entrusts to us, the more liberty we grant people." Spiritual Authority by W. Nee, p. 121

OUR PRACTICE: In nearly every conference or training we observe a declaration of authority. Old Testament cases of disobedience are cited, death and negativism are ascribed to any who do not agree and respond positively. Is this not an insidious form of control?

4. THE CHURCH ground implies that we are open to receive and accept all genuine believers. We should not demand certain practices or separate those who have a different feeling about matters not of the "faith."

OUR PRACTICE: Those who have any reservation about any of our practices are "unclear", "do not see the vision" and remain outsiders. Our ways are "God given" and our practices are, "God ordained." This implicitly condemns all (those in the church or outside of it) who don't fully embrace them. In this way we have thoroughly isolated ourselves from all other Christians.

5. Do not SEPARATE or make a distinction between the saints who may hold a different feeling about matters of form or practice.

OUR PRACTICE: Those who express reservations about the latest way or practice are regarded as "old", "in death", "negative", "not clear", "pouring cold water", "blowing cold winds" and are set aside as far as the "Lord's up-to-date move" is concerned.

6. There should be OPEN fellowship, in an atmosphere which allows all saints to "speak the truth in love."

OUR PRACTICE: Speak about and report only the "positive." Support whatever is being promoted, speak well of it, even inflate the statistics; meanwhile ignore any fact or evidence which shows a weakness or a failure. Of course in this way we never have a failure. Loyalty and blind approval is prized while objectivity and honesty are strongly disapproved. Whoever stays "positive", and confirms everything is "in", and is often elevated, while those who speak their genuine concern are regarded as "negative", and "undermining" and soon privately and perhaps publicly condemned.

7. There should be no effort to ORGANIZE or UNIFY the churches.

OUR PRACTICE: Constant pressure is applied through trainings, videos, and slogans to push churches and saints to conform. Elders are belittled, as being "old", "ambitious", "big-speakers", and "undermining", if they do not bring their churches into conformity. LIFE LESSONS & TRUTH LESSONS are promoted as the only way to properly express the truth and help new believers.

(These are some of the aspects that caused me to leave the denomination years ago.)

8. Do not get involved in "HOW TO", or in the promoting of ways. The natural always wants to know "how to." This will only produce behavior and outward form. It is not the way of life. Life will issue from the abiding and this will produce organic fruit.

OUR PRACTICE: In recent months, messages and books are flooding us with "THE WAY TO…" There is a "way" and a "how to" given for whatever we do or say. The saints are learning now only how to behave but are put in the realm of policing others, especially the elders, so all freedom is lost.

9. The Lord's GOAL IS THE CHURCH. Whatever we do must be for the building up of the church. The ministry exists not to build up itself but the local churches. "If God's people could only see that the object of all ministry is the founding of local churches and not the grouping of Christians around any particular individual, truth, or experience or under any particular organization, then the forming of sects could be avoided. We who serve the Lord must be willing to let go our hold upon all those to whom we have ministered, and let the fruits of our ministry pass into local churches governed entirely by local men." The Normal Christian Church Life by W. Nee, p 91.

OUR PRACTICE: There is very little time or energy for building up the local church. Time, money, and resources are constantly exhausted in order to defend, protect, supply, build up, and "meet the need" of the ministry by "serving the ministry in the ministry's way." Videos, conferences, trainings, and standing book orders have all become necessary to "keep current with the ministry."

10. We MEET in the name of the Lord. All the saints have the freedom to share as the Spirit gives them utterance.

OUR PRACTICE: Everyone is measured by whether they speak "the ministry." Truth Lessons, Life studies, and foot-notes are proper ways to speak or express anything. The safest way is just to read with little or no comment. Surely this is CONTROL, and must offend the headship of the One in whose name we meet. In The Normal Christian Church Life, p. 92-93 Bro. Nee warns: "Whenever a special leader, or a specific doctrine, or some experience, or creed, or organization, becomes a center for drawing together the believers of different places, then because the center of such a church federation is other than Christ, it follows that its sphere will be other than local. And whenever the divinely-appointed sphere of locality is displaced by a sphere of human invention, there the divine approval cannot rest. The believers within such a sphere may truly love the Lord, but they have another center apart from Him, and it is only natural that the second center becomes the controlling one. It is contrary to human nature to stress what we have in common with others; we always emphasize what is ours in particular. Christ is the common center of all the churches, but any company of believers that have a leader, a doctrine, an experience, a creed, or an organization as their center of fellowship, will find that that center becomes the center, and it is that center by which they determine who belongs to them and who does not. The center always determines the sphere, and the second center creates a sphere which divides those who attach themselves to it from those who do not."

"Anything that becomes a center to unite believers of different places will create a sphere which includes all believers who attach themselves to that center and excludes all who do not. This dividing line will destroy the God-appointed boundary of locality, and consequently destroy the very nature of the churches of God." Brothers I beg you, I plead with you, please consider objectively; is this not our case? Is this the reality of the vision that caught us, and is it still clear and pure? Is there a possibility that while we condemn, "poor Christianity", that we are like Laodicea, saying, "I am rich…and do not know that we are… poor and blind…? May the Lord find room in our hearts to extend His mercy, that we might repent. Perhaps we might be rescued and restored to His blessing.

Albert Zehr
Burnaby, B.C.,
Canada

"A thing that is useful may be useful for some and not for others, but a thing that is true remains true for all people and beyond the end of time."
J. Gresham Machen

www.ingramcontent.com/pod-product-compliance
Lightning Source LLC
Chambersburg PA
CBHW051149120626
46547CB00012B/1005